W9-BGN-590

PRINCIPLES

OF

NEGOTIATING INTERNATIONAL BUSINESS

PRINCIPLES
OF
NEGOTIATING
INTERNATIONAL
BUSINESS

Success Strategies for
Global Negotiators

Lothar Katz

www.negintbiz.com

Copyright © 2008 Lothar Katz
All rights reserved.

ISBN 1-4196-9503-7

Booksurge Publishing   Charleston, SC, U.S.A.

To order additional copies, please contact
www.booksurge.com
1-866-308-6235
orders@booksurge.com

To contact the author, please e-mail lotharkatz@negintbiz.com

To Annette:

I want you to know that I am eternally grateful for your strong and loving encouragement, as I have been during the last twenty-eight years. I love you.

Table of Contents

Preface

Who Should Read This Book

Principles of Negotiating International Business is for any-one seeking to boost his or her success in international nego-tiations. This may include businesspeople negotiating with counterparts in or from other countries, students who are in-terested in preparing for future challenges, and others with a general interest in the subject. While our perspectives are inevitable influenced by our own cultural background, we will try to maintain a neutral perspective that makes the in-formation valuable to all readers, no matter what their own cultural background might be.

The information given in this book focuses on professional business negotiations. That includes interactions large and small, from preparing multi-billion-dollar corporate merg-ers and acquisitions to engaging with small local distribu-tion companies. We do not necessarily cover typical tourist interactions, such as bargaining in a street market or hag-gling over the price of a cab ride. Street merchants and other vendors in foreign countries, especially in third-world and emerging economies, often resort to extreme negotiation techniques that might be considered inappropriate within the local business culture. We chose to focus on practices that people are likely to use in business settings.

This book is not for the novice. If you are unfamiliar with the fundamentals of effective negotiation and have little or no negotiation experience in your own country, we encourage you to check out some of the *References* listed on page 177.

How To Use This Book

Part I, **International Negotiations**, describes how culture impacts negotiations, explaining which factors influence how members of a given cultural group prefer to negotiate. We also take a close look at the framework and structure of the international negotiation process, reviewing each of the phases that negotiations go through.

No matter what your experience level, we urge you to read at least Chapters 2, 3, 4, and 6. Without understanding the fundamental cultural concepts that explain the difference between international negotiations and domestic ones, negotiating with people from other cultures will be left to chance and you rarely get the best deal you could.

Part II, **Negotiation Techniques Used Around the World**, lists numerous techniques negotiators around the world commonly use. While many of these may also be applied in domestic negotiations, we discuss each in its international context, reviewing

- how the technique works,
- how to counter it,
- who likely uses the technique,
- who will not likely use the technique,
- when using the technique may be effective, and
- when using the technique may not be effective.

Even experienced negotiators can increase their effectiveness through identifying and leveraging the most powerful international negotiation techniques.

Where to Go For More Information

Principles of Negotiating International Business is actually part of a larger offering. While it gives a comprehensive overview on the principles of negotiating internationally and using negotiation techniques effectively across borders, it provides only limited information about specific countries and cultures. At the same time, one of the most important rules of negotiating effectively in cross-cultural settings is that you must have a comprehensive understanding of your own cultural values and practices, as well as those by which your counterparts are influenced when their cultural background is different from yours.

What we offer you to obtain this kind of country- and culture-specific knowledge is an on-line addendum to this book, called **Country Sections**. At

www.negintbiz.com/cs

you have the opportunity to download these country-specific documents (in PDF format) for each of 50 countries around the world.

These Country Sections are typically between 5 and 10 pages long, which makes them easy to print and take along on business trips. Each of them provides extensive information about the subject country, following the same format as Chapters 3 through 7 of this book: Relationships; Effective Communication; Initial Contacts and Meetings; Negotiating and the Bargaining Exchange; Agreement, Closure, and Execution. In addition, they include suggestions for females negotiating in the country or males dealing with local female counterparts, as well as other information about the country that may be helpful when negotiating business there.

If you prefer having all information in one place, we have a great alternative for you: the complete content of this book plus the full set of 50 Country Sections as described above are included in another book in the series called

Negotiating International Business -
The Negotiator's Reference Guide
to 50 Countries Around the World.

Also published by BookSurge, LLC, the book is available from online resellers such as Amazon.com and many bookstores.

Definitions: Regions of the World

As long as cultural stereotyping is avoided, it can be helpful to refer to groups of countries or geographic regions if the majority of their people share certain values and behaviors. Keeping in mind that there remain important cultural differences between members of each group, we occasionally use the following terms throughout this book:

- *Arab countries* refers to the Gulf Arab countries of Bahrain, Kuwait, Oman, Qatar, Saudi Arabia, the United Arab Emirates, and Yemen, as well as the Levantine Arab countries of Lebanon, Syria, and Jordan.

- *Middle East* refers to all Gulf and Levantine Arab countries, plus Egypt, Iran, Iraq, and Israel.

- *Europe* includes the Eurasian border countries, such as Russia, Ukraine, and Turkey.

- The *Nordic countries* or *Nordics* are Denmark, Finland, Iceland, Norway, and Sweden. We sometimes refer to their people as *Northern Europeans*. The three countries of Denmark, Norway, and Sweden may also be referred to as *Scandinavia*.

- *Southern Europe* refers to several of the European countries around the Mediterranean Sea, namely Cyprus, Greece, Italy, Malta, Portugal, Spain, and Turkey.

- *Slavic countries* refers to Belarus, Bulgaria, Croatia, the Czech Republic, Macedonia, Moldova, Poland, Serbia, Slovakia, Slovenia, Russia, and Ukraine. The countries of Albania, Bosnia and Herzegovina, Hungary and Romania are not Slavic but may show cultural similarities.

- *Latin America* in the context of this book refers to all countries on the American continents with the exception of Canada, Mexico, the United States, and the numerous countries of the Caribbean Islands. We always use the term *Latin Americans*, rather than simply saying *Americans*, when referring to the population of these countries. This choice of language reflects our attempt to keep with terms most readers can easily recognize. It means no disrespect to people from Latin America, who may be quick to point out that they are Americans, too.

- We use the term *Americans* to describe those citizens and residents of the United States who, to a large degree, share distinct cultural values and preferences, such as individualism, achievement orientation, a sense of urgency, directness, and a distrust of formal authority.

A large group of people in the United States are either first-generation immigrants, or they grew up in one of the country's many subcultures, such as the sizeable Hispanic community. While these residents usually blend in well, they nevertheless often hold on to a different set of values. Without meaning disrespect to this or any other group, the term *Americans* as used in this book does not include these individuals.

Part I: International Negotiations

Chapter 1: Take On The Challenge

The Stakes are High, and so Is the Risk

Watch a few old *James Bond* movies, and you may come away thinking that cultural differences are no big deal. In the secret agent's world, natives of all countries speak English with only a trace of a local accent (unless, of course, they are Russian), most people seem to prefer British or American manners and etiquette, and except for a few folkloristic customs here and there, everyone readily understands even the most subtle expressions and gestures.

Experienced business travelers know that the real world is not like that. While countless people around the globe speak at least some English, language gaps still can be huge barriers. Manners and etiquette vary greatly across cultures, and their influence on the way people perceive others is often substantial. Entire business deals have dissolved solely because company representatives spoke or behaved in ways deemed inappropriate within their host culture. Many a negotiator has failed to reach agreement or to achieve the desired results because they did not prepare well for these and many other challenges of doing business in foreign countries or with foreign representatives.

This mistake can become incredibly expensive. The potential impact of international negotiations to the strategic and financial success of a company is hard to overestimate. Whether the goal is a product sale, a turnkey project, a licensing agreement, a BPO (business process outsourcing) engagement, a joint venture, a service contract, or any other kind of business deal, two factors can make negotiating across cultures a high-risk undertaking:

- *The financial stakes are high.* Since the outcome of an initial negotiation often determines the strategic position of a company in a particular country or region of the world, failure to reach agreement hugely impacts factors such as market access, resource availability, or required financial investments.

- *Most companies' cultural competence when engaging in a new territory is low.* Few or none of their executives and middle managers may have a sufficient understanding of effective negotiation approaches in the 'new' country's culture, which substantially reduces the odds of winning great deals and reaching favorable terms.

Cross-cultural negotiations combine high stakes with high risks, which creates a powerful incentive to learn how to 'make things happen' the right way. Competitive pressures in many international markets have increased considerably over the past decades. Countries whose economies were historically either closed or were accessible to only a few foreign players have become level playing fields, attracting trade partners from all around the world. Success in this competitive environment often requires differentiating oneself by adjusting to local mentalities and cultures. It is no surprise that businesspeople who are good at crossing cultural boundaries, such as many British, Dutch, and Singaporean negotiators, tend to achieve superior outcomes in global trade negotiation.

Some argue that the effects of globalization have mostly eliminated the need to prepare for cultural differences. To support this position, they may emphasize that more people than ever have extensive international experience, or they might point to the numerous brands and icons of popular culture, from retail chain Starbucks Coffee to singer Britney Spears, who managed to establish a global presence with a huge following in many different countries. We believe that these arguments are misleading. Studies have shown that instead of disappearing, disagreements in cultural values among employees in different country subsidiaries of multinational companies are usually more pronounced than those between employees working for domestic companies in these countries. This indicates that people who had greater opportunity to learn about other cultures may cling on to their own one more strongly as a result. Globalization might cause cultures to look alike on the surface, but it would be dangerous to conclude from these disappearing clues that the fundamental cultural differences themselves, as manifested in people's values, beliefs, and attitudes, are also disappearing.

The Impact of Culture on Negotiations

Many definitions for the term *culture* have been given. Yet, none seems comprehensive enough to express its full meaning. We favor the very practical approach proposed by MIT professor Edgar H. Schein: "Culture is the way in which people solve problems." It captures the essence of why international negotiators need to understand cultural differences: the art of negotiation is the art of problem solving, which in itself is strongly influenced by the values, beliefs, attitudes, and behaviors that are shared, albeit to varying degrees, among the members of each cultural group. Disagreements over these factors often lead to cross-cultural conflicts that could seriously jeopardize the success of a negotiation. Adding to the challenge, we find upon closer inspection that *every* aspect of the negotiation process is subject to these influences and may take on a different meaning within the framework of a given culture:

- *Why negotiate?* In western business cultures, the primary purpose of negotiating is to 'make a deal.' Without the goal of engaging in a business agreement with clearly defined objectives, Westerners rarely consider negotiations meaningful. In contrast, many Asians may negotiate with the primary objective of building relationships and creating long-term alliances, even if the specific items being negotiated seem insignificant.

- *What to negotiate?* A wide range of different items can become the subject of negotiations. People from achievement-oriented cultures (refer to page 38), such as Americans or Canadians, tend to concentrate on tangible benefits when assessing the value of negotiated items or concessions, for example the price of a product or the cost of a service. Members of ascription-oriented cultures, for instance Indonesians or Colombians, may also be focusing on non-tangible benefits, such as the status that comes with forming a large partnership or the prestige of winning an important foreign customer. In order to obtain such benefits, they may be willing to accept terms outsiders to their cultures might view as unfavorable.

- *When to negotiate?* Timing and pace of negotiations can be a source of frustration for both sides. People from strongly relationship-oriented cultures, such as Venezuelans or the Japanese, may be unwilling to engage in serious business negotiations unless they already know their counterparts well and have had ample opportunity to develop relationships with them. If not, it could take several trips and many months before the core negotiation can begin. In contrast, negotiators from those task-oriented cultures whose members consider business relationships less critical, for instance Americans or Australians, may frequently attempt to speed up the process in order to 'get quick results.' These attitudes create conflicting objectives and often lead to tensions in the negotiation process. In extreme cases, talks may break down before the parties have even started conducting serious negotiations.

- *How to negotiate?* This is where approaches vary the most across cultures. There can be vastly different concepts of how a negotiation should be conducted. Protocol and formality, negotiation styles and tactics, bargaining and haggling exchanges, the way agreement is reached and documented, and many other rules and behaviors may differ in very fundamental ways. People in some cultures may insist on bargaining sequentially, going down a list item-by-item; others prefer a parallel multi-item bargaining approach that looks at the deal holistically. Some will openly share relevant information, willingly putting their cards on the table; others may play them close to the chest, revealing as little as possible about their motives and objectives. Some use logical reasoning to persuade their counterparts; others may prefer appeals to emotions and intuition. The list of potential issues is long. Many of these disagreements are hard to reconcile.

What makes these differences crucial is that most human beings hold a deep-founded belief that 'their' way of doing things, which is rooted in the preferred concepts of their culture, is the better one – or worse, the *only* acceptable one. The resulting spectrum of how people belonging to different cultures define 'proper' and 'improper' behaviors spawns an array of pitfalls that may be difficult to recognize even for very experienced negotiators.

Effectiveness in international negotiations requires a profound understanding of cultural influences, not a mere application of rules. A checklist of do's and don'ts alone, no matter how extensive, will not be enough to master tricky situations. Successful international negotiators have learned to leverage four essential competencies:

- They understand the values, beliefs, attitudes, and behaviors that are *relevant* in their counterpart's culture.

- They use, as well as recognize and counter as needed, negotiation techniques that are *effective* in the culture.

- They are familiar with culture-specific behaviors that are *important* since they stimulate a positive negotiation outcome.

- They know to avoid behaviors that could be *damaging* and might wreak havoc with the negotiation because of cultural incompatibilities.

There is much more to know about any of the world's cultures than this book has room to address. Our mission is more modest: we focus on those aspects that determine culture-specific relevance, impact, importance, and damage avoidance in international negotiations.

A few popular culture guides seem to imply that you must strictly follow local etiquette whenever you conduct business in another country. Experienced international negotiators know that this is untrue. In today's global world, people in all but the most rural places understand and often tolerate the fact that foreigners act and behave differently. In France, people may make fun of you behind your back if you use a fork with your right hand instead of with the left. Simply ignore it and focus on your business objectives instead. In Argentina, conversations may stop around you if you start chomping ice. Realize something is wrong and stop doing it, but do not worry about the impact the 'incident' might have on your business relationship. In Japan, you may cause a moment of embarrassment if you walk into a traditional restaurant with your shoes still on. Your local counterparts will be quick to stop you, politely asking that you take them off. Apologize, laugh with the Japanese group, then forget about it. This mishap will not affect your negotiation either. In each of these situations, people may be irritated at first but will quickly conclude that it was just an odd or funny incident. However, there is a critical line you must not cross: you must never speak or behave in ways that signal disrespect for people or culture.

Being odd will often be forgiven. Being rude, rarely.

Rudeness may lie in seemingly little things. Brazilians' feelings might be hurt if you gave them a brochure printed in

Spanish rather than in Portuguese, the country's language. Indonesians may consider you aggressive and impolite if you keep frequent eye contact, which to them signals disrespect. Arabs may be seriously offended if you handed them something with your left hand, which Muslims consider unclean. Even though your perceived rudeness may reflect no bad intentions whatsoever, it could critically damage the progress of your negotiation. As an outsider to a culture, it is your responsibility to avoid behaviors its members define as offensive. Unfortunately, it can be difficult to distinguish between behaviors that may just be considered odd and those that are viewed as rude. Several factors influence this:

- Locals who are experienced in dealing with foreigners are usually more tolerant than those who have little or no cross-cultural experience.

- People living in big cities may be more relaxed about cultural faux pas than those living in rural areas.

- People in positions of high authority can be less forgiving than ordinary peasants usually are.

- Younger people may mostly ignore unusual behaviors, while older ones could be very strict.

- People in countries whose population is very diverse, such as the United States, usually tolerate a much wider spectrum of behaviors than those living in very homogeneous cultures, such as Japan.

- If your counterparts know that you are visiting the country for the first time, they may be much more forgiving than if you had many previous visits or if you actually lived there.

- In addition, individual beliefs and preferences unrelated to culture can also be strong influence factors.

Focusing on the essentials for business success, we strive to provide relevant information on how to successfully conduct international business negotiations but cannot address all differences in manners and etiquette that are potential sources of conflict. If you are unsure whether the people you will be negotiating with are sufficiently experienced in interacting with other cultures and tolerant enough to forgive minor faux pas, we recommend that you familiarize yourself with the local etiquette of the country or countries you plan to visit. Several useful guides for this purpose are listed in the *References* and *Useful Websites* sections at the end of this book.

The Competent International Negotiator

Success in international negotiations is not limited to individuals with a specific personality or style. However, the following characteristics and behaviors, all of which can be learned and developed, are typical of highly effective cross-cultural negotiators:

- *Competent international negotiators know themselves.* Understanding one's values and preferences is critical when trying to bridge cultural gaps and reach agreement in foreign countries. Successful individuals know how directly or indirectly they communicate, how important business relationships are to them, to what extent they are willing to trust people with whom they have had only limited business interactions, how competitive they are, how they make decisions, and so on. Knowing themselves enables them to leverage their greatest strengths and overcome their shortcomings at critical junctures during the negotiation process.

- *Competent international negotiators realize that cross-cultural knowledge is vital to their success.* Looking beyond generalizations such as 'all humans are created equal,' they recognize how the historic, economic, social, and cultural environment in which members of a cultural group grow up affects values, behaviors, and practices. Accordingly, they familiarize themselves with relevant aspects of a potential business partner's culture before making initial contact. Having learned to recognize cultural differences, they are able to identify sensitivities and potential areas of cross-cultural conflict, which greatly improves their ability to negotiate productively and successfully.

- *Competent international negotiators understand the risks and benefits of stereotyping.* Generic cultural information is inevitably based on stereotypes, describing aspects that may be typical of a given culture but not necessarily of any of its individual members. Effective cross-cultural negotiators know that assumptions about their counterparts that are not based on first-hand experience can be dangerous and may cause substantial communication problems and disagreements. Individuals who believe that 'Arabs haggle all the time,' 'the Japanese never make individual decisions,' 'Russians are always aggressive when negotiating,' or that 'a German's word is as good as a contract' may rely on these assumptions when dealing with individuals from one of these cultures. However, they may find themselves in trouble when dealing with real Arabs, Japanese, Russians, or Germans, realizing too late that the people they are dealing with could have little in common with such stereotypical models.

Negotiators who have mastered the challenges of working across cultures avoid this mental trap. They realize that stereotypes can be valuable if based upon validated research and statistically relevant findings, but only when used as a collective description of typical values, preferences, practices, and behaviors within a society or group of people. No matter how accurate a stereotype about such a group may be, it might not apply at all to some of its individual members.

Competent negotiators therefore use stereotypical information only as a starting point when dealing with individuals from a given culture, as a set of assumptions that they are prepared to question and modify continually. They realize that adjusting their own behaviors to the cultural stereotypes may help initially since it will likely put their counterpart at ease and reduce the risk of cultural misunderstandings. At the same time, these effective negotiators remain open minded and frequently adjust their approach as they learn more about the other's individual characteristics and preferences.

Cultural stereotypes can be powerful tools helping negotiators prepare for cross-cultural interactions, but only if used right. Assuming that someone is indeed an 'average American' or 'average Chinese' is dangerous. Assuming that the person *is likely* to share practices and preferences with that fictitious 'average American' or 'average Chinese,' however, while remaining fully aware that the person could in fact turn out to be very different from the stereotype, is a sound use of cultural stereotyping.

- *Competent international negotiators continuously demonstrate respect.* Not shy in pursuing their interests and in remaining firm where appropriate, they will miss few opportunities to demonstrate that they respect their counterparts, never letting ego get in the way of negotiating. They know that negotiating is not about outsmarting or outmaneuvering the other party and understand that the end result is much more relevant than the way to get there. Most importantly, great cross-cultural negotiators are humble. They refuse to take themselves more seriously than they take the deal they are trying to close. Accordingly, they never dig in their heels and strive to show appreciation for the other party's beliefs and positions throughout the negotiation exchange.

Demonstrating respect for the other side includes acquiring knowledge and showing curiosity about the other's country and culture. Before meeting a foreign counterpart for the first time, effective cross-cultural negotiators might learn a few facts about the other country's history and cultural background. When applicable, they will learn some of the language, realizing that knowledge of at least some of its words and phrases will be greatly appreciated. Having no ambition to be 'cultural judges,' they never question the legitimacy of either side's values. In addition, they never openly criticize the other's country, even when counterparts may do so themselves.

- *Competent international negotiators are flexible and adaptable.* Knowing themselves and understanding their counterpart's cultures well, they are able to identify gaps and can decide how to bridge them effectively. Without having to blend perfectly into the other culture, successful individuals manage to expand their own cultural comfort zone enough to keep their counterparts at ease. They know when it is ok to follow their own preferred approaches, when it is better to play by the other side's cultural rulebook, and when to compromise somewhere between the extremes. They are also prepared to adjust to the numerous factors other than culture, such as socio-economic background, family, religion, schooling, and many others, that may influence others' values and practices. With counterparts who are less adaptable, this knowledge and attitude put them in control of the negotiation process and greatly improve their chances of achieving their objectives.

Smart negotiators always maintain credibility and integrity *as viewed by their counterparts.* In cross-cultural settings, this may require much flexibility, adjusting to the other side's standards and practices without sacrificing their own values. In some countries, it could mean negotiating in a straightforward style and staying away from deceitful and distractive tactics. In others, bargaining may be viewed as a game and negotiators might win the locals' respect by skillfully demonstrating their mastery of deceptive negotiation without losing their integrity. The key to success in international negotiations is adaptation, not transformation.

- *Competent international negotiators refuse to make assumptions about their counterparts' intentions.* They internalize the most important rule in international business, which is never to take anything personally. Instead of simply assuming that an apparently unfriendly remark or behavior reflects negative intentions, they go to great lengths to verify proper communication and identify cultural misunderstandings. In addition, they are unwilling to take things at face value. For example, they will not take a counterpart's poor grammar or pronunciation as an indication of limited intelligence, nor will they assume a lack of interest if a counterpart comes ill-prepared to a meeting. If in doubt about the other party's intentions, effective negotiators choose not to assume anything. Instead, they usually ask or otherwise try to learn more about their counterparts' true objectives.

- *Competent international negotiators are persistent and patient.* Different cultures may have vastly difference concepts of how much time to spend in each of the phases of negotiations. American's motto might be 'time is money' while their Arab counterparts may believe that 'haste is of the devil.' Successful negotiators are willing to allocate whatever time they need to accomplish their objectives, working through excessive bureaucracy, stalling tactics, slow decision cycles, and other obstacles as needed. Persistent enough to move the negotiation process as swiftly as possible, and patient enough to accept it to be as slow as necessary, they realize that both traits are equally valuable.

- *Competent international negotiators prepare well.* This includes all aspects of the negotiation process itself, but also factors peripheral to the negotiation that could become distractions and hindrances. Examples for this kind of preparation are obtaining proper travel documents and visas, preparing and aligning their negotiation team to ensure consistency and maximum impact, bringing information material and background documents that may prove useful during the negotiation exchange, and so on. Thus prepared, negotiators can focus all their energy on the success of the negotiation itself.

Chapter 2: Preparing for International Negotiations

> **Key Concepts: Negotiating, Bargaining, and Haggling**
>
> *Negotiating* includes all phases of an exchange designed to establish agreement between two or more parties over the provision of goods, services, financial incentives, or other benefits. The negotiation process ends when all related transactions between the parties have been completed. It could extend over a considerable time period, sometimes many years after the parties signed a contract.
>
> *Bargaining* is a process of exchanging offers in order to negotiate the terms of a purchase, agreement, or contract. Accordingly, it represents one of the phases within the overall negotiation process. The offers made in the bargaining exchange constitute promises to provide tangible or intangible individual items, such as products, materials, properties, services, payments, warranties, or deadlines. Commonly referred to as concessions, these offers are usually contingent upon receiving certain benefits in return.
>
> *Haggling* is defined as extreme bargaining and often includes repetitive patterns of small incremental requests or offers. Partners in international negotiations may unfortunately not agree on what the term 'extreme' means in this context. People in haggling-averse cultures such as Sweden may consider more than three subsequent offers for a particular item as excessive, even if each represents a significant improvement over the previous one. In contrast, cultures whose members enjoy haggling, such as Saudi Arabia, may consider ten or more such iterations as normal bargaining, even if each offers only a small improvement.

Phases of Negotiations

All domestic or international negotiations go through six major phases. As they move from one phase to the next, and often at major junctures in-between, experienced negotiators will track pre-defined milestones that serve as progress indicators, adjusting their tactics and concessions as necessary.

- *Preparation.* During this phase, both sides analyze context and boundaries of the negotiation, define their objectives and non-settlement alternatives, and plan their approach. This includes selecting strategies and tactics that support the negotiation objectives, planning timing and size of individual concessions, defining an exit strategy, and more. Throughout their preparation, effective negotiators also strive to learn as much about the other party as they possibly can.

- *Relationship Building.* Structure, duration, and relative importance of this phase are hugely culture-dependent. In some countries, the existence of close relationships is not a necessary precondition for doing business together, so this phase may include little more than brief introductions and some background checking. In other cultures, businesspeople may not be willing to enter into any serious bargaining without first getting to know their counterparts well and establishing strong links. Here, the relationship building process could take many months and require several meetings. This phase generally starts with the initial contact between the negotiating parties, which in many cultures can be critically important for their future interactions.

- *Information Gathering.* During this phase, negotiators seek to understand the other side's intentions, objectives, and goals. They will also strive to find out about the value their counterparts are assigning to the individual items being negotiated and the concessions they are prepared to make. Since objectives and value assessments are often poorly aligned between the parties, it is common for resistance and conflicts to emerge during the information gathering phase.

- *Bargaining and Decision-Making.* Depending on the negotiating parties' preferences and cultural practices, bargaining and decision making may represent separate phases or they might blend into one. Negotiations over multiple items are often characterized by iterative exchanges that move back and forth between bargaining and decision-making. The bargaining phase starts with one side making its opening offer, which is usually followed by alternating concessions, offers, and counteroffers between the parties. With some cultures, this exchange might include frequent haggling over single or multiple items.

  Decision making is also subject to strong cultural influences. They frequently determine who will be involved, which factors to consider, and how much time to spend in the decision-making process. Once both negotiating parties have indicated that they are close to reaching agreement, additional bargaining over remaining differences may be required in order to reach consensus and advance the negotiation to its final phases.

- *Closure.* The closure phase begins when both negotiating parties believe that they have reached agreement. It usually ends when they sign a formal contract. Depending on the parties' preferences, creating this document might already start during the bargaining exchange, using the draft contract as a protocol to keep track of interim agreements. Levels of detail included in its final version can range from high-level, capturing only the essential aspects of the agreement, to very detailed, with specific provisions for many cases and eventualities. The act of signing the contract may be a mere formality to some, while a very important step for others. Members of some cultures, for example Americans, distinguish strictly between the intentions of the final agreement and the provisions spelled out in the contract, often insisting that only the latter be considered binding. Others, for instance most Arabs, expect the spirit of the agreement to be upheld even when the contractual terms only loosely reflect it. Many such aspects are strongly influenced by cultural orientations.

- *Execution.* In the absence of other provisions, executing a contractual agreement normally starts shortly after its signature. This phase may include follow-up steps to exchange additional information, communicate progress, or clarify details. Both sides are then expected to implement their commitments as spelled out in the contract and/or agreed upon during closure. How accurately these commitments must be met in order to be considered satisfactory again varies across cultures.

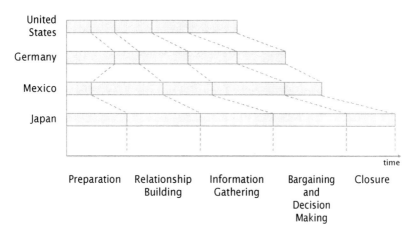

Figure 2.1 Comparison of negotiation phase durations in different cultures.

The overall length of the negotiation process and the time spent in each of its phases vary greatly. It is influenced by a number of factors, such as the parties' sense of urgency, how far apart their original objectives were, or how well their negotiation styles align. Cultural influences could also be substantial, as illustrated in Figure 2.1. It shows a qualitative analysis of how much time members of different cultures may be spending in each negotiation phase. This cross-cultural comparison is stereotypical and will not necessarily apply when actually negotiating with individual representatives from any of these cultures. It is interesting to note the variance in typical phase lengths, though. For instance, Americans, with their high sense of urgency, and Mexicans, with their relatively high acceptance of uncertainty, tend to spend much less time preparing for negotiations than German or Japanese businesspeople usually do. The latter commonly share a propensity for detailed analysis. On the other hand, Americans and Germans are usually willing to enter into serious negotiations without first getting to know the other party well, a concept that is frequently rejected by Mexican and Japanese businesspeople who allow substantially more time for relationship building. The Japanese may also spend extensive time gathering information before the bargaining exchange can begin.

We should emphasize that the structure of the negotiation process may not be as sequential as implied by the phase descriptions and by the segmentation shown in Figure 2.1. Many negotiators, especially members of highly polychronic cultures (see also page 79) who usually prefer a holistic approach to negotiating, may repeatedly move back and forth between the information gathering and bargaining phases before making any decisions. People from some countries may even re-open the bargaining exchange during the execution phase of a negotiation, when a contract has already been signed. Relationship building and information gathering tend to happen in parallel in many countries, for instance in Japan.

Context and Boundaries

Negotiating business deals with foreign counterparts requires a thorough understanding of the political, legal, economic, corporate, and cultural context and boundaries both parties are subjected to. Without such knowledge, there will be a substantial risk of missing aspects critical to the negotiation or even finding oneself in a 'mission impossible' after spending considerable time and effort. Let us take a look at each major factor:

- *Political environment.* Nowhere in the world are companies able to conduct international business independently of their countries' political situation. Governments frequently seek to influence large business deals in order to protect and enhance their country's political or economic strength, technological know-how, or infrastructure. Bureaucracies tend to present major hurdles even if a country's political climate is generally pro-business. They can become stifling when governments intend to keep strict control of local markets. Changes in political power may prove disruptive if existing business arrangements conflict with the new leaders' objectives. In addition, a lack of political stability may raise valid concerns over the long-term viability of business agreements, as is currently the case in countries such as Russia, Ukraine, Indonesia, or Thailand. Support from government offices, trade organizations, and independent consultants around the world often proves valuable when assessing these aspects.

- *Legal environment.* In countries where governments promote open business and free trade, legal regulations and restrictions can nonetheless represent serious impediments to business negotiations. Many an international negotiator has been taken by surprise when a counterpart informed them that what they proposed was actually illegal in the country. For instance, exclusive distributor agreements, common in many regions of the world, may be against the law in the European Union. Price discrimination across different groups of customers, another practice that is accepted in many countries, is unlawful in the United States, where companies are banned from using such business practices not only domestically but worldwide. Legal considerations often impact contractual aspects, too. A contract may be void if written in the wrong language, as is the case with English-only documents in the French-speaking Quebec province of Canada. Oral commitments could prove legally binding in Germany. Many such legal pitfalls exist. It is strongly advisable to work with legal experts who are well-familiar with applicable laws and regulations.

- *Economic environment.* Foreign exchange procedures, currency valuations, and general stability of markets are among the key factors to consider when assessing the potential value of an international business deal. Cross-border business arrangements regularly require financial transfers through foreign exchanges, which are typically controlled by central banks. It is vital to understand the procedures and commercial banking constraints governing this process. In addition, currency fluctuations, caused by inflation, general economic instability, or by outside factors such as shifts in the world's financial flows and systems frequently affect business arrangements. A deal that might have looked attractive at the time the contract was signed could become very unfavorable should rates of exchange change significantly. It is essential to assess possible future currency fluctuations and consider their implications for potential deals.

- *Corporate environment.* Strategic direction, market focus, level of international experience, size and available resources, corporate values and attitudes, and many other factors influence objectives, strategy, tactics, and styles of international business negotiators. Proper preparation for negotiations with another company includes finding out as much as possible about it, both at the strategic level and in areas that relate directly to the negotiation process. It is crucial to understand the type of agreement the potential partner is seeking: is the primary goal to close a contract or to nurture a business relationship? Is the focus on short-term gains or on long-term benefits? Similarly, it will be advantageous to identify the key stakeholders in the negotiation that is about to begin: who is going to be at the negotiation table, who will make important decisions, and who might be influencing them? In addition to direct company contacts, customers, suppliers, partners, former employees, industry analysts, and others may be valuable sources for this kind of information.

Understanding the ground rules the negotiating parties are willing to play by is of equal importance. One such rule might address confidentiality requirements. If sensitive information must be revealed over the course of the negotiation, the parties may prefer to close formal nondisclosure agreements (NDAs), or they could choose to rely on verbal assurances of confidentiality. Either way, it will be important to clarify both sides' commitments up-front.

- *Cultural environment.* As we already saw in Chapter 1, the values, behaviors, and practices that are unique to each country's culture wield powerful influences on all aspects of the negotiation process. Their implications are usually harder to identify and prepare for than those of any other contextual negotiation factors. Before familiarizing oneself with a specific culture, it is important to understand how culturally homogeneous a country's population is. *Homogeneous* cultures, among them many Asian, European, and Latin American countries, tend to tolerate a relatively narrow spectrum of 'acceptable' behaviors and practices. Cultural minorities in these societies are often pressured to adjust to the majority's cultural rules. In contrast, many culturally mixed countries exist. *Pluralistic* societies include population groups whose individual cultural norms differ in significant ways, which may either be largely tolerated across the groups, as is the case between Belgium's Flemings and Walloons, or which might be the cause of much friction and aggression, such as in Indonesia. *Heterogeneous* societies, whose cultural influences from a variety of inhomogeneous population groups may be very diverse, usually tolerate a wide spectrum of styles and practices. Examples of the latter include Israel, Switzerland, and the United States.

When preparing to negotiate with people in or from another country, it is important to know whether its culture is homogeneous, pluralistic, or heterogeneous as this influences negotiation styles and tactics. Homogeneous and pluralistic cultures tend to impose several cultural taboos on their members. In pluralistic countries, these taboos may differ greatly between the individual cultural groups. That could make it necessary to prepare for all of them, unless it is safe to assume that all counterparts all belong to the same cultural group. Heterogeneous cultures tend to tolerate a wider range of styles and behaviors. Nevertheless, these societies usually also hold up strong values that may impose stringent requirements with which foreigners are expected to comply.

Key Concepts: Corporate versus Cultural Influences

The corporate environment and the cultural context of a negotiation show several interdependencies. Policies, procedures, and practices of most companies are influenced by the cultures of their country of origin. Since multinational corporations frequently standardize their value systems and procedures on a worldwide basis, one might expect their employee base to be fairly homogeneous across national and cultural boundaries.

However, it appears that ***corporate influences*** are able to moderate ***cultural influences*** only to a small degree, if at all. In fact, researchers have found that cultural influences tend to become more pronounced among employees working for companies of foreign, rather than domestic origin. One possible explanation for this phenomenon is that pressure on employees to conform with standardized organizational norms provokes a 'cultural resistance' aimed to protect local cultural values and practices.

This finding has significant consequences for international negotiators. For instance, if a negotiation with another company is set to include employees from different cultures, it will be vital to factor each counterpart's specific cultural influences into the preparation instead of assuming that a similar approach will work with all of them.

Essential Preparation Steps

To vary a famous quote by Thomas Alva Edison, "Success in international negotiations requires one percent inspiration and ninety-nine percent preparation." Indeed, the worst mistake anyone can make is to arrive at the negotiation table with no more than a perfunctory understanding of motives, objectives, expectations, and attitudes of both negotiating parties. Surprisingly, it is not uncommon to meet people who do just that: relying on their ability to 'figure things out as they go,' they spend little time preparing before engaging in international negotiations. Some of them may not realize that this makes them easy prey when dealing with competent counterparts.

As a smart negotiator, you know better than to make this mistake. Here are the six crucial steps that will get you ready for even the toughest international negotiation:

• ***Identify your BATNA.*** The *Best Alternative To Negotiated Agreement*, or BATNA, describes the most favorable non-settlement option that will still be available to you should you fail to reach agreement with your current counterparts. This could mean making a similar deal with another partner or otherwise engaging in business interactions that support your original strategic objectives. Few negotiations ever take place in which one side has no realistic alternative to reaching agreement, which tends to leave them in an extremely weak position.

Knowing your BATNA is important and becomes crucial in certain situations, for instance when a counterpart tries to exert strong pressure to close a deal. The BATNA will determine your options throughout the negotiation. For example, it will allow you to decide whether to accept the deal you are being offered or to walk away if those are your only alternatives. Identifying the BATNA requires brainstorming all available options, evaluating each of them, and selecting the one that is most attractive. Next, you should try to find ways to improve this option in order to identify your strongest possible BATNA. As a general rule, the more attractive it is, the stronger your overall negotiating position will be.

• ***Define your objectives.*** Business negotiators commonly pursue multiple objectives. These may include price targets, payment terms, warranty conditions, service arrangements, and many others. You must clearly define each of your objectives, setting your aspirations high and preparing to defend them through strong arguments if challenged by a counterpart.

Next, categorize your objectives. You may consider some of them essential, others as important, again others as desirable. There could also be some you might be indifferent about. Be realistic and honest when determining which is the case, since this matters when planning your approach. Items you consider essential tend to become strong negotiation levers for the other party if they learn about this fact, so do not make the mistake of classifying too many items in that category. Once your objectives are clear, consider substitutes. Would you be willing to trade one important item for another? If so, under what conditions? Having considered such aspects upfront may give you an edge during the bargaining exchange. Make sure to verify that your resulting objectives are indeed better than your BATNA. If not, why engage in the negotiation at all? You should also determine your Least Acceptable Result (LAR) which represents the minimum overall value of the deal you are willing to accept: is it the same as your BATNA, or will you only accept a deal that provides you with a higher value? If so, by how much?

- *Understand 'the other side.'* To maximize the success of your negotiation, you will need to learn everything you possibly can about your counterparts. What is the other party's BATNA? What are its objectives, strengths, and weaknesses? Which potential issues that could arise because of conflicting attitudes and objectives can you identify upfront? In addition, you should identify all of the stakeholders who will participate in your counterparts' decision process. Who will you be negotiating with directly, who will you be negotiating with indirectly, and who else might be influencing decisions? Is the final decision going to be made by a single person or by a group? If the latter, is it likely to require consensus? Knowing the answers to all of these questions will become relevant when defining your negotiation strategy.

The initial preparation phase is only the starting point to acquiring the necessary knowledge about the other side. You should continue this pursuit throughout the relationship-building, information gathering, and bargaining phases.

- *Plan your cultural approach.* Other important aspects are to verify your own understanding of the other side's culture and to carefully assess how 'locked into their culture' your counterparts are. Businesspeople in remote regions of underdeveloped countries may have very little experience with other cultures. With such counterparts, learning enough to command a working understanding of their culture may be your only promising option. While pulling in an advisor to close some of the cultural gap may help, this is rarely enough to achieve true collaboration. Your business partnership will likely remain frail in such a constellation.

In contrast, company employees who regularly deal with international partners or who work in a multinational environment may have adjusted to a more 'international' style of conducting business. While this will not eliminate principal cultural differences, the negotiation could include a mix of styles and practices, some of which may be reminiscent of local habits with others following widely practiced American or European business styles. Nevertheless, a general rule for international negotiations is that whoever is most 'conversant' in the other's culture will have a powerful advantage: their ability to influence decisions improves greatly, and they can employ styles and tactics from either side's cultural context.

Negotiating from that position, you can continually modify and adjust your style as appropriate. While you may often find it advantageous to embrace the other's cultural script, you always retain the option to explain that 'things are done differently' in your own culture. As long as you avoid violating strict cultural taboos, you can thus introduce your own styles and practices and leverage them to your advantage.

Insisting on your own cultural style, either because you lack the required cross-cultural understanding or because you believe you are negotiating from a position of power, is a dangerous proposition. If you are lucky, your counterparts come better prepared than you and may therefore be able to close the cultural gap. This will give them a valuable advantage, though. Otherwise, it will be left to chance whether or not anything comes out of the negotiation at all. Either way, you are unlikely to walk away with the best deal you could possibly get.

- *Define your negotiation strategy.* The first step to defining your strategy is to analyze the strengths and weaknesses of each of your own objectives as well as those of the other side. Could your counterparts use some of your essential objectives as pressure points against you in order to obtain significant concessions? Such threats must be factored into your strategic approach. At the same time, you may be able to identify opportunities. For instance, can you leverage some of your counterparts' essential objectives in a similar fashion? In addition, can you identify items they will likely care about much more than you do?

  You must also consider many other factors that are often influenced by cultural aspects. For instance, you will need to carefully decide what negotiation styles to employ, how to use your main bargaining levers of power, information, and time most effectively, for example when sizing and timing concessions. We will discuss these aspects in greater detail in Chapter 6.

- *Define your exit strategy.* What are you going to do should the negotiation appear to lead nowhere? Will you be able to end the negotiation without leaving negative feelings on either side? If not, are you willing to burn your bridges with your counterparts, and have you considered the implications this fact may have on your ability to do business with others in the country? All of these questions need to be answered prior to making contact with a potential business partner. More often than not, asking them when you reach a standstill in the negotiation will be way too late and the damage might already be irreversible.

Team Negotiation

Preferences vary across cultures when it comes to team negotiation. For example, while Americans are often more inclined to 'go it alone,' arguing that this approach ensures consistency of strategy and is more efficient overall, the Chinese almost exclusively negotiate in teams and will usually employ groups of several negotiators. As a general rule, group-oriented cultures, among them most Asian and Latin American countries, tend to equate the size of the other side's team with the importance attributed to the negotiation. If a foreign party sends only a single individual or a small team to negotiate, their local counterparts may take this as a lack of interest in and commitment to building a dependable business partnership. Some may even refuse to enter into any serious negotiations under such circumstances.

Independent of cultural views, negotiating in teams in international settings has several other advantages. It allows bringing in and matching up different functional experts, ensuring that the right level of expertise is available when needed and fostering relationships between specialists on both sides who are usually quick to find common ground despite their cultural differences. In addition, well aligned teams are more likely to achieve their objectives since they can leverage greater experience and use a broader set of negotiation tactics to their advantage. Among others, the Chinese and the Taiwanese are usually very effective team negotiators.

Team members need to be assigned specific roles to optimize their contributions to the negotiation process, such as:

- Team Leader or Facilitator
- Technical Expert

- Trade & Logistics Expert
- Legal Expert
- Cultural Expert / Relationship Builder

Selecting team members requires careful consideration of several factors. While functional expertise plays a role, other aspects are often more relevant when selecting team members for international negotiations. General negotiation experience and specific cultural understanding weigh strongly, as do the individuals' interpersonal skills, dependability, patience, persistence, and risk propensity. They also need to be focused on the negotiation objectives and willing to work hard to ensure alignment with their other team members. Shrewd negotiators tend to use disagreements among their counterparts to their own side's advantage.

Depending on their cultural background, some negotiators may also consider it important that rank, status, or age of team members on both sides match. Even if such expectations may seem irrelevant in one's own culture, it will be wise to address them when deciding how a team should be composed. Including an outsider on the team, for instance or independent consultant or someone from another part of the company, may also prove valuable. Such individuals often find it easier to keep a neutral and emotionally unbiased perspective of the status and progress of negotiations. In certain cultures, it may be beneficial to provide team members who do not belong to the same company with a business card designed to conceal that fact.

Executing a negotiation strategy as a team requires more than putting the right people in the right roles. It is of equal significance to prepare the team well, ensuring complete alignment between its members before the negotiation even starts. It is strongly recommended to practice different scenarios through role plays in order to prepare team members for tactics to use and for those that the other side is likely to employ. In the heat of the bargaining exchange, it will be much harder to reach this kind of alignment. However, it is best to interrupt negotiation in order to realign a team if disagreements surface among its members or if one of them is blundering. This is strongly preferable to bringing up such observations in front of the other party. Otherwise, its members might use the situation to play team members against each other.

In most settings, effective teams consistently achieve better negotiation results than effective individuals. The benefits of spending time upfront to prepare the team well are often significant and can be substantial.

Key Concepts: Individualistic versus Group-Oriented Cultures

Several intercultural researchers have conducted studies to analyze cultural preferences across a spectrum ranging from strong individualism to strong group orientation. They found that members of *individualistic cultures*, for instance Americans, Anglo-Canadians, Australians, or the Dutch, tend to place significant emphasis on individual interests and independence. While most of them value relationships with others, these are rarely viewed as an essential requirement for conducting business. People from these cultures usually also prefer individuals to make decisions. They may accept group decisions only if they view them to be in their own best interest.

In contrast, members of *group-oriented cultures*, for example the Chinese, Indians, Indonesians, Mexicans, or most Latin Americans, tend to value their group's collective beliefs and practices much more highly. Examples for such groups are the person's family, their social network, their work team, a larger organization they belong to, or the society they live in. To them, strong and dependable relationships are often critically important, both in their private lives and in business. Decision making in this culture is usually a collective process that may require reaching consensus among all group members.

Most cultures combine elements of both orientations, albeit to a varying degree. Preferences for individualism versus group orientation influence several aspects of the negotiation process, from team composure to relationship building, decision making, or general timing of phases and concessions.

Chapter 3: Relationships

Before we analyze the importance of relationships in business, let us define the term: in our context, 'relationship' describes interpersonal connections between two negotiating parties, which could be companies or individuals, that

- allow the individuals involved in the negotiation process to become familiar with each other,
- establish and nurture trust between them,
- promote win-win cooperation based on mutual benefit, and
- increase the parties' willingness to do business together, even if doing so involves significant risk and uncertainty.

How Relationships Impact Negotiations

It seems intuitively obvious that the strength of relationships between negotiating parties will significantly influence the outcome of negotiations between them. Human experience dictates being more careful when dealing with strangers with whom no relationship exists than with people we know and trust. Accordingly, strong relationships between the negotiating parties usually reduce the tension between them, bring balance and stability to the process, help both sides focus on the benefits of the exchange, and increase their dedication to overcome obstacles. The impact depends to no small degree on the negotiators' cultural background, though. Four different categories classify the importance of relationships for the negotiation process in a given culture:

- *Moderately important.* Members of cultures belonging to this group, which includes Americans, Australians, Austrians, Canadians, Germans, and a few others, rarely view strong relationships a necessary precondition for business interactions. Being task-oriented, they tend to focus on business objectives and contract clauses. Their primary motivators are often near-term financial or strategic benefits rather than long-term relationship aspects. Though they may expect to get to know the other party better while doing business together, they do not need to trust someone in order to make a deal with the person. Many in this group are reluctant to invest significant time and effort into relationship building during the early stages of business engagements. Negotiation styles and attitudes in these cultures do not depend much on relationship aspects. In addition, business ties exist mostly at the corporate level: if a new company representative is introduced into an existing business relationship, that person is usually soon accepted as a valid partner.

- *Important.* These cultures tend to value trust between business partners more highly than those in the previous category do. While they may also engage in negotiations without first getting to know their counterparts, members of this group will strive to learn much more about them over the course of the exchange. Once initial negotiations have been successful and trust has been established, a sense of loyalty may develop, facilitating future business engagements. Relationships still mostly exist at the corporate level with this group, but individual employees commonly also aim to strengthen personal ties with their business counterparts. These characteristics apply to many European cultures, among them Finland, France, Hungary, Northern Italy, Poland, Switzerland, the United Kingdom, and others.

- *Very important.* People in this group of cultures, which includes Indians, Hong Kong Chinese, Koreans, Mexicans, Pakistanis, Russians, Saudi Arabs, Southern Italians, Spaniards, most Latin Americans, and many others, value lasting and trusting business relationships. They strongly prefer to do business with those they know and like. Accordingly, they are prepared to spend significant time building and strengthening relationships. Usually not interested in near-term deals, they mostly focus on longer-term engagements and repeat business. Because potential business partners may first have to prove themselves trustworthy, initial engagements could be small, especially with foreigners. When members of this group engage in business interactions without first spending time to get to know their counterparts, this likely indicates that they are aiming for quick gains and are not interested in doing business with the other party in the long haul. The concept of corporate relationships does not mean much to this group. Since business is viewed as personal, individuals expect to spend considerable time and effort to develop close ties with their immediate counterparts even when their companies have a long history of doing business together.

- *Critically important.* Members of cultures belonging to this group, among them Asian countries such as China, Indonesia, Japan, Malaysia, the Philippines, and Taiwan, as well as countries such as Brazil, Egypt, or Greece, prefer to build deep and lasting relationships with prospective partners before entering into serious business engagements. They may expect to continue developing such relationships into true friendships as the business partnership continues. Both sympathy and trust are essential requirements for them to make deals with others.

In cultures where relationships are critically important, foreign negotiators often find it extremely difficult to reach business agreements if such agreements might adversely affect the other side's existing relationships with other parties. The prevalent business attitude in these cultures is that current partners must first be given opportunities and receive support that might allow them to win the deals the new party may be proposing. It may be only if these partners decline such an opportunity that the proposing party will be given serious consideration.

With this group, it is vital to be prepared to spend considerable time and effort building strong relationships throughout the negotiation process without appearing too focused on any agenda. With the exception of the Japanese, who seem equally focused on tasks and relationships, members of this group may appear less task-oriented than others may. They do not pay much attention to contracts, since most of them believe that the strength of business relationships matters much more than 'a piece of paper' does. Keeping in touch with them on a regular basis even after the negotiation exchange has ended will ensure that commitments are kept and opens doors for additional business. Since they mostly focus on long-term engagements and repeat business, decision makers may agree with initial deals that appear unfavorable for them, expecting their new partners to make up for this down the road. People in this group pay little attention to corporate-level connections, since few of them believe that business relationships can be successful without strong personal ties. While the more pragmatic among them may also engage in business interactions with relative strangers if the prospects are sufficiently attractive, members of this group will most likely focus on short-term benefits and might not shy away from taking unfair advantage of the other party when given a chance.

These characterizations provide several clues as to what to expect and where to focus when conducting business with people from foreign countries. However, these categorizations should never be taken at face value, since they apply mostly in business areas that do not critically depend on personal relationships. In some industries, such as banking, financial services, or legal counseling, the nature of business interactions requires strong trust between the parties irrespectively of their cultural background. Such a requirement may promote different practices in these industries. In any case, spending time and effort to build closer relationships in international interactions is always conducive to business and therefore strongly recommended, regardless of cultural background and type of business.

Westerners seeking to engage in international business in Africa, Asia, Latin America, and in Southern Europe often underestimate the impact of strong personal ties on the success or failure of negotiations. Experienced international negotiators realize that the number of countries where people view relationship building as very important or critically important far exceeds that of cultures who view them as less relevant. They adjust their behaviors and actions accordingly, realizing that failing to meet the expectations of a member of a strongly relationship-focused culture would make that counterpart unlikely to commit to any business deals.

Note that the categories we defined apply only to business relationships. Away from business, people may have different concepts of what constitutes relationships. For instance, Americans are often said to be 'easy to get to know, hard to get close to.' In business and elsewhere, they tend to be friendly but are often very selective when it comes to developing close friendships. In contrast, Austrians and Germans can be hard to get to know personally, especially in business situations. Away from business, though, many of them develop large networks of close friends with whom they may build strong and dependable relationships.

Showing Respect

Successful businesspeople know that showing respect for their negotiation partners is essential. In cross-cultural situations, the importance of demonstrating, by word and deed, esteem and regard for the other party only grows further. Counterparts who feel disrespected are likely to look for ways to 'make the other pay' for that, which tends to trigger emotional decisions and reduces the effectiveness of the negotiation. In strongly relationship-oriented cultures, seemingly small incidents might actually cause the negotiation process to break down completely if handled poorly.

Respect is expected at different levels. While all humans expect to be respected as individuals, most of them also want the organizations and institutions they represent, and their country and culture as a whole, to enjoy proper regard and appreciation. In individualistic culture, personal respect tends to be of utmost importance. In strongly group-oriented cultures, showing apparent disrespect for an organization or society may represent an even greater offense than treating individuals with less than the expected consideration and courtesy.

What people respect and what constitutes 'proper' respect are complex culture-specific concepts which are influenced by several factors. One of them is whether the respect members of a given culture are willing to pay another person more strongly depends on ascription or on the person's individual achievements.

Key Concepts: Ascription versus Achievement

In *ascription-oriented cultures*, for instance in most Asian and Latin American countries, people tend to focus on family background and hierarchical rank when assessing a person's importance and the respect he or she deserves. While those in positions of authority may be respected regardless of their personal shortcomings, individuals who have achieved significant personal successes but lack the 'right' background and rank might command little respect in these cultures.

In contrast, members of primarily *achievement-oriented cultures*, such as the United States, Canada, or Australia, much more appreciate individual accomplishments. They may respect business achievements, personal wealth, public recognition, and education irrespectively of a person's background and upbringing.

Another aspect that is specific to the cultural context is how much respect people expect to be shown. This depends largely on whether the culture's status orientation is primarily egalitarian or authoritarian.

Key Concepts: Egalitarian versus Authoritarian Cultures

People in strongly *egalitarian cultures*, among them Australians, the Dutch, Israelis, and Scandinavians, expect every person, regardless of his or her role, to be treated with respect and courtesy. They prefer flat hierarchies and may have little tolerance for individuals who think themselves superior to others. Authority is often informal, and respect depends much more on individual characteristics than on ranks or titles. Foreign senior executives may actually enjoy greater respect when downplaying their own role than if trying to signal status and importance.

Strongly *authoritarian cultures* view clear hierarchies as essential in business and elsewhere. Titles and degrees are generally respected in these cultures. Executives may enjoy enormous deference and tend to behave in paternalistic ways. They are expected to demonstrate their importance through status symbols and corresponding behaviors. Being overly friendly with people of lower rank can be counterproductive with this group of cultures, which includes Brazil, Greece, Indonesia, Malaysia, Pakistan, the Philippines, Saudi Arabia, Thailand, and others.

The concepts discussed so far are characterized by a focus on individual concerns. Violating any of the implied rules may disturb relationships with the affected individual but does not necessarily impact the interaction with others. However, respect often also represents a collective concept, especially when dealing with cultures that highly value group harmony.

**Key Concepts: Harmony, the Concept of Face,
and the Influence of Pride**

Many cultures, especially group-oriented ones, are characterized by a strong preference for maintaining **harmony** across their members. This value is often reflected in the practice of individual embarrassment leading to collective shame. With some groups, corresponding behaviors may include wording concerns in positive and constructive ways or refraining from commenting on people in front of others. However, other societies, in particular many Asian ones, have little tolerance for any kind of negative communication and impose much stricter cultural rules. Symptoms of such strong harmony orientation may include evasive answers when people disagree with comments or requests, problems that are not openly confronted or even acknowledged, or statements that only reflect what the speaker believes a counterpart wants to hear, rather than what he or she really thinks. Members of these cultures often view direct communication as disrespectful.

Closely related to this orientation is the concept of **face**, which prevails in most Asian countries. *Face* is the external representation of a positive and harmonious self as viewed by others. The term's use is not limited to individuals; rather, families, groups, organizations, or even whole nations may have *face* in this sense. *Loss of face* can either be caused by own actions and behaviors deemed inappropriate within the culture, or by the actions of others. For instance, openly showing emotions may be viewed as a lack of self-control and can cause *loss of face* in some cultures, as can being treated disrespectfully by another person or group.

Pride is different from *face* inasmuch as it represents an internal value that depends on individuals' views of themselves. Nevertheless, since the perceptions of others strongly influence people's pride, this makes little difference in terms of cultural norms and accepted behaviors. Similar to the concept of *face*, pride may also be individual or collective. Expectations of proper actions and behaviors in countries where pride tends to play a significant role, such as in Spain, Mexico, or Latin America, resemble those of *face*-oriented cultures.

Causing an individual or a group to lose *face* or hurting someone's pride may have severe implications for relationships, even if done inadvertently. Since seemingly small infractions of cultural rules could jeopardize and even disrupt important negotiations, it is vital to respect these concepts, adjusting behaviors as necessary.

Effective Relationship Building

To feel closely connected with a business counterpart, most humans require three factors to come together: they need to know the individual well, like the person, and trust him or her to a comfortable degree. Accordingly, effective relationship building is stimulated by the following behaviors:

- *Allow your counterparts to get to know you.* As a general rule, the less your negotiation counterparts know about you, the more likely they will be to act cautiously, conceal their intentions, and slow the negotiation so they can gather further information. When considering the effectiveness of the immediate negotiation as well as its long-term implications, you will often find it to be in your best interest to share more information about yourself than you might otherwise view necessary. In fact, while negotiators in some countries only care to know about aspects that are immediately relevant to the negotiation exchange, members of many other cultures expect to learn seemingly immaterial details about their counterparts. They might seek to receive personal information, for example about your family background and education, understand your company's background and history, and get insight into your professional role and responsibilities. In some cultures, even highly personal questions, such as whether you are married or whether you have plans for children, are deemed acceptable. This interest is generally stimulated by your counterparts' desire to understand your values, beliefs, and preferred behaviors. It would be unwise to reject outright such questioning. In addition, your counterparts may inquire about your negotiation objectives and intentions. Whether or not they really expect you to share much of this information depends on the specific cultural context.

- *Nurture liking and empathy.* When dealing with cultures whose members strongly value relationships, whether or not your counterparts actually like you and feel good around you can make a substantial difference to their negotiation attitudes as well as their willingness to make concessions. Beyond showing respect, being open and sociable often promotes stronger liking. As with other cross-cultural aspects, playing by your counterparts' cultural 'rulebook' rather than by your own one will be vastly more effective. For example, some Westerners may be tempted to loosen up and show their personal side as a way to nurture liking. Members of other cultures, especially authoritarian ones, could view this approach as intrusive and disrespectful, even with close business partners. In many situations, it is wiser to maintain an air of restraint and formality around them while avoiding the appearance of being impersonal. Another example of culture-specific assumptions is that 'likeness creates liking,' which is not necessarily the case. For example, while most Americans value similarity and tend to bond more strongly with people with whom they share common interests, the French value difference and may warm up to people whose experiences and interests lie in different areas than their own ones. As a general rule, try to focus on what your counterparts value and enjoy, not on what might make yourself most comfortable.

Social events often create great opportunities to develop closer ties. Declining invitations to such events without giving *very* compelling reasons can be disastrous for the relationship building. A common way for people in many cultures to stimulate the process is to consume alcoholic drinks together. The Chinese, the Japanese, Koreans, Russians, and Ukrainians are somewhat notorious with this regard. No matter what your personal preference, it is generally recommended to participate in after-hours drinking in these cultures, since not joining in will be viewed as a sign that you are not interested in building closer relationships. However, avoid getting overly drunk, since this may again be held against you. If you are unwilling to drink alcohol, your best bet will be to claim medical reasons for this refusal. Doing so may nevertheless adversely affect your relationships.

- *Build trust.* Interpersonal trust depends on many influence factors. One of them is age: younger people are generally less mistrusting than older ones. Other factors depend on cultural context. Task-oriented people, among them many Americans, Australians, Austrians, Canadians, or Germans, base their trust mostly on competence and behavioral consistency. With them, you may establish and nurture trust by demonstrating that you are competent in your field, making realistic commitments, and consistently honoring such commitments or at least showing good intentions to do so.

  Relationship-oriented people, on the other hand, focus more strongly on predictability. When negotiating with an unknown party, they value recommendations from others whom they already trust and will look for examples of past behavior that may indicate how dependable the potential new partner is. You will often find it easier to establish initial trust through third parties who can introduce you and give references. Regular communication and follow-up will be taken as indication of your continuous commitment to the business partnership. In addition, demonstrating your willingness to 'go the extra mile' by making unexpected efforts to support your counterparts will nurture their trust in you.

Levels of trust in unknown people differ substantially between cultures. In a cross-cultural survey, researchers have found that about two-thirds of people from Northern Europe or from China, and about half of the Americans surveyed, agreed with the statement that 'most people can be trusted.' In contrast, less than one in five Brazilians, Turks, or Romanians shared this belief. Accordingly, it may actually require substantially more effort and dedication to win people's trust and confidence in some cultures than in others.

Opportunities for relationship building abound around international negotiations. They include business meetings and conferences, lunches and dinners, business entertainment, social events, and many other occasions. Whether making small talk, meeting in formal settings, attending ceremonial banquets, or socializing at informal gatherings, always treat the event as an opportunity to deepen relationships with the other party. However, keep in mind that you will be more effective if you act in ways that are consistent with your counterparts' cultural expectations *in the particular setting*. Bringing up the wrong subjects during small talk, appearing too casual in meetings, failing to follow the rules of etiquette at banquets, or inappropriately bringing up business topics at social functions are all significant faux pas that could weaken the critical relationships you may be trying to build.

Gender-Specific Aspects of Relationship Building

In recent years, women's emancipation in business has fortunately made much progress in many countries around the world. Though a lot more may need to happen to achieve equal representation, it is unquestionable that more women than ever now fill professional roles and carry substantial responsibility. In spite of this general trend, building and nurturing effective business relationships across genders remains challenging in many countries and cultures. Two factors tend to get in the way:

- *Lack of concepts for business relationship building across genders.* Clear frameworks exist in all societies to determine how relationship building is conducted among men in business. However, such concepts often do not apply to males and females conducting business together, which complicates working across genders. Men in particular often behave differently when dealing with women, which tends to make the relationship building process harder and less effective.

- *Traditional expectations of female roles.* Men in several cultures may still hold on to traditional views of the roles women should fill and how women should behave around men. Western ways of doing business may clash with these beliefs. In countries such as Japan or Saudi Arabia, men may not be prepared to deal with women in business at all unless the women fill subordinate roles. Lacking a framework for dealing with women who hold substantial responsibility and make important decisions, they could behave awkwardly when dealing with such women. Chances are that some of them might avoid interactions altogether. In other authoritarian or patriarchic societies, for instance in Egypt, Indonesia, Greece, Spain, Turkey, or in many Latin American countries, men might be a bit more forthcoming. Nevertheless, many of them still openly or secretly disapprove of women filling what they view as 'male' roles. Accordingly, businesswomen often remain relative outsiders in these cultures. It can be difficult for them to win the trust and respect of their male counterparts. Paradoxically, relationship building can be particularly challenging for women in many of the cultures whose members value relationships most strongly.

As a result of these factors, building close relationships in international negotiations tends to be easier for male negotiators than for female ones. While this may appear –and indeed is– unfair, visiting businesswomen may have to realize and accept that they might not be able to build close business relationships with some of their male counterparts in such countries, even if they are willing to make special efforts in order to prove themselves as likeable and trustworthy partners.

Chapter 4: Effective Communication

Language

In today's global environment, English has become the *lingua franca*, the almost universal language of the business world. By and large, the challenges presented by language differences are much less significant than they were only fifty years ago. Nonetheless, language barriers may still prove to be substantial obstacles in cross-cultural negotiations.

Even when interpreters are readily available, being able to speak the language of negotiation counterparts or teaming up with someone who does may create significant benefits. For one, speaking the same language strengthens relationships, since it tends to make people more comfortable with each other. On top of that, some of the information conveyed inevitably gets lost in translations. Languages commonly reflect concepts that are tied to their cultural context. Many of them lack certain words that could be important in another party's cultural framework. In addition, translations inevitably lose important clues, such as speech patterns and tone of voice that signal authority or indicate that someone is lying. Using interpreters should therefore be a last resort only if no viable alternative exists.

Even when one party is able to speak the other's language, one must remain aware of the risk of misunderstandings. Research has shown human communication to be ineffective even between native speakers of the same language. Translation inaccuracies, mispronunciation of words, and other lapses that are common when people communicate in a foreign language inevitably add further confusion and miscommunication.

Interacting with Non-native Speakers

Here are a few suggestions to help improve the communication across parties whose native languages are different:

- *Listen attentively.* Following the line of thought of a person speaking in a language that is foreign to the speaker can be hard, even if it happens to be your native language. You should generally pay closer attention in such situations than you might normally do when communicating with people in your own country.

- *Verify mutual understanding.* Because misunderstandings are frequent, giving and seeking feedback are very important in non-native language communication. Acknowledge frequently what is being said, and ask your counterparts to confirm their understanding whenever appropriate.

- *Use simple language, speak clearly, and slow down.* Unless you are talking in the listeners' native language, they may be struggling to identify and translate what you are saying. This process tends to be much slower than the speaker might assume. Choosing simple words, pronouncing them clearly, and slowing the speed of your speech will greatly improve the odds of being understood. If a foreign counterpart asks you to repeat something you said, do not conclude that they did not hear you. More likely, you may have used an expression unfamiliar to the person, or you may have talked too fast for the individual to cope with the required translation. Repeating what you said in a louder voice could only make the person uncomfortable without necessarily solving the problem. It will be more helpful if you repeat your message using different words and speaking more slowly.

- *Pause frequently.* Translating takes time. Even when counterparts seem reasonably fluent in a foreign language, they will be struggling to keep up with the message if you speak at normal speed in your native language. Pausing frequently will give them the time to understand and reflect on what is being said.

• *Repeat yourself and use visual aides.* You will frequently find that repeating important points is helpful in getting your messages across. Using visual aids is but one way to accomplish this: if what you say and what you show convey the same points, your chances of being understood improve considerably. For the same reason, provide handouts during your meetings and follow up with clear and easy-to-understand written summaries.

Non-Verbal Messages

Humans use gestures and other 'body language' to emphasize points or to send subtle messages. Some of these non-verbal messages may be intentional, while others are based on subconscious behaviors that are hard to control. The meaning of such messages is understood by most members of the person's cultural group, often also by others. For instance, most Westerners take smiles or nods of the head as indication of agreement, folded arms as disbelief or rejection, head scratching as a show of surprise or confusion, or fingers drumming on a table as a sign of impatience.

Unfortunately, only a few such clues are familiar to people all around the world, such as sitting straight, frequently blinking the eyes, or suddenly speaking in a higher pitched voice, which may all indicate that the person displaying the behavior is telling a lie. Most non-verbal messages are not universally understood, though. Greeks and Turks may read nods of the head as rejection. Asians tend to smile not only to express positive emotions, but also to conceal annoyance or anger. Other non-verbal messages may mean little or nothing to Westerners. For instance, some Asians inhale sharply when trying to indicate a serious problem. Others may look down while speaking with another person as a show of respect. Since gestures tend to be small and subtle in Asia, Westerners might miss some of them entirely.

Non-verbal communication can get even more complicated if gestures or behaviors take on different meanings across cultures. The American *OK* sign, with thumb and index finger forming a circle, is an obscene gesture in several countries. Slapping the open hand over a fist, which Americans and Canadians sometimes do to signal a passion for action, might be taken as a huge insult in Russia or Ukraine. Keeping frequent eye contact conveys sincerity in some cultures, while people in others may interpret the same behavior as rude and intrusive. Moving closer to another person in conversation may signal intimacy or mere friendliness. In contrast, moving away may be read as a sign of respect for a counterpart's personal space by some, while others could take it as an indication of discomfort that is caused by them.

Learning to use and interpret body language correctly is essential in any culture. Of equal importance is the ability to follow the other culture's implicit rules. For example, most Asians restrict their body language and disapprove of the extensive gestures that Italians, Spaniards, Mexicans, Latin Americans, and others may prefer. Asians also often consider touching others a major offense, even between people of the same gender. While the relevance of such non-verbal communication varies across cultures, getting it wrong can have disastrous consequences for relationships and negotiation outcomes alike.

Directness

A common cause of intercultural communication problems is how directly or indirectly people express themselves. Here are a few typical statements illustrating different styles:

Direct Communication	Indirect Communication
'We cannot do this.'	'This may be difficult.'
'Your proposal is unacceptable.'	'We need time to think about it.'
'This is not correct.'	'This is an interesting perspective.'
'This cannot be done today.'	'We will see.'
'I'm just calling things what they are.'	'We must be respectful of others.'
'Yes' means 'I agree.'	'Yes' means 'I heard what you said.'
'We will consider it' signals interest.	'We will consider it' signals skepticism or rejection.
'No' indicates rejection.	'No' is rarely used.

It is a popular misconception that *indirect* represents the equivalent of *vague*. The contrary is true: it is possible to communicate very clear messages in a highly indirect fashion. However, most Westerners require extensive practice to learn this skill.

In addition to subtle verbal clues such as in the above examples, people in indirect cultures often use other ways to communicate their real message, making it important to 'read between the lines.' What is *not* being said often becomes more important than what *is*. For instance, if a person praises an insubstantial aspect of a proposal that has just been made, the real message may be that he or she dislikes essential parts of it. Silence is another, non-verbal way to communicate displeasure and rejection.

Several factors influence how directly people communicate, such as whether a culture is generally more individualistic or group-oriented, egalitarian or authoritarian, comfortable or uncomfortable with uncertainty. Typical levels of directness vary widely across cultures. The Dutch, Israelis, or people from the northeastern United States tend to be very direct, leaving little uncertainty in their statements. The British, Canadians, the French, or Americans from other parts of the country are usually fairly direct, though less so than the first group. Koreans, Mexicans, and most Latin Americans use more indirect communication and generally prefer subtlety over frankness and candor. The Chinese, Indonesians, Thais, and above all others, the Japanese tend to communicate in a very indirect manner that can be difficult for Westerners to interpret correctly.

It is characteristic of most societies that their members tend to view their own culturally preferred style as superior to others. People from direct cultures can get very frustrated with those communicating more indirectly, sometimes accusing them of being indecisive, evasive, or even sneaky. Similarly, members of cultural groups who value indirect communication may be shocked, feeling insulted or attacked by foreigners who communicate much more directly. As a general rule, it is usually easier for people from direct cultures, among them most Westerners, to adjust to more indirect ways of communication than the other way around. This is because they are generally familiar with the concept of diplomacy. In contrast, most Asians find it very difficult to be even nearly as blunt and outspoken as people in the West can be.

Levels of directness influence many aspects of international negotiations. Here are a few suggestions for Westerners preparing to interact with members of highly indirect cultures:

- *Do not force disagreement.* Always phrase offers and proposals in ways that will allow the other side to reject them without having to give a straight 'no' answer. Ask open questions and be prepared to propose alternatives rather than making take-it-or-leave-it statements.

- *Reject tactfully.* Respond with non-committal phrases if you dislike an offer or proposal. This is usually more effective than if you rejected it right away, since you will avoid offending your counterpart and also retain the option to change your mind later. Alternatively, make a counterproposal without commenting on the one your received, or simply ignore it altogether.

- *Be sensitive.* Listen carefully for subtle messages and watch your counterparts' body language for small clues.

- *Refrain from making assumptions.* Never assume that there is agreement because nobody said 'no.' Confirm agreement by asking the other side what they are willing to do.

- *Do not worry too much about the clarity of your message.* Westerners dealing with Asians, most of whom prefer indirect communication, often experience discomfort if things are 'left up in the air,' as they may see it. Fearing that subtle messages they previously conveyed may not have been properly understood, they often prefer to provide summaries at the end of meetings that clearly list issues and concerns. In reality, it is much likelier for Westerners' communication to lack the required subtlety than to be too indirect when dealing with Asians.

- *Avoid confrontation.* If the bargaining exchange becomes heated or when the negotiating parties get tied up in a dispute, it will be even more important to match your counterparts' communication style. Realize that in the heat of the argument you may be more inclined to communicate in a straightforward style while your counterparts will likely take this more negatively than they might do at other times.

Using Technology to Communicate

It should be obvious that using technology when communicating across cultures is intrinsically less efficient than speaking with a person face-to-face. Media such as e-mail, web conferencing, and various kinds of online collaboration tools come with significant shortcomings. They block out body language and reduce opportunities for immediate feedback and clarification. In addition, they force what members of strongly relationship-oriented cultures usually view as impersonal communication: since they cannot see or hear their counterparts, they lose their sense of connectedness that affects communication and decision-making. Phone calls and conferences usually work better but still impose many restrictions. Even when using videoconferencing equipment, the only available technology that supports both verbal and non-verbal messages, subtle messages frequently get lost and participants tend to communicate more indirectly than they might in relaxed face-to-face settings.

As a general rule, how to use technology to communicate with a negotiation counterpart depends mostly on the importance and strength of the relationships. When communicating with people who highly value relationships, it is vital to find or create opportunities to meet with them whenever possible. Otherwise, it is best to use the phone. Until strong bonds have been established between both parties, the use of e-mail and other media should be restricted to exchanges of information or summaries of previous conversations. With members of cultures focusing less on relationship aspects, e-mail or web conferencing will generally prove effective. However, it will still be advisable to create opportunities to speak with counterparts face to face.

Making it Work

Communicating across cultures has been described as a minefield of practices, preferences, rules, and taboos that can be very difficult to cross. Nevertheless, anyone sensitive and flexible enough can make it work if they follow the right approach. Here are a few points to keep in mind for your next international negotiation:

- *Study the rules.* What members of a given culture consider appropriate or inappropriate may often appear arbitrary. Find enough information about your target culture's rulebook upfront to know what people expect.

- *Recognize communication preferences as cultural preferences.* How people in a given culture view the world determines to a large degree how they communicate. Learn enough about your counterparts' culture, and you will find it easy to communicate with them.

- *Realize that common language can be deceiving.* As Americans and the British have frequently discovered, speaking the same language does not mean that people share the same values and practices. In fact, meeting foreigners who are completely fluent in your own native language can mislead you to ignore cultural differences. Avoid falling into this mental trap by reminding yourself of the cultural differences if necessary.

- *Keep an open mind.* The hardest part of communicating across cultures can be to refrain from making assumptions about your counterparts' intentions. You will succeed if you make it a rule for yourself to verify any and all of your assumptions by seeking feedback and obtaining additional information before jumping to any conclusions.

Chapter 5: Initial Contacts and Meetings

Making Contact

Once you have assessed the environment you will be negotiating in, learned as much about the other party as you could, identified your BATNA, defined your negotiation strategy, and done everything else you needed to in order to be well prepared, the crucial next step will be to make initial contact. The most important decision at this point will be whether to contact the other party directly or through someone else. In some cases, there may be dependable existing contacts with the other side that could be leveraged. Otherwise, using third-party intermediaries is generally preferable, since such individuals could provide several valuable services:

- *Open doors.* Local intermediaries may be able to leverage existing relationships to make contact with a targeted company. In countries where relationships are critically important, it can be very difficult to get access to the right people without such contacts. In some cultures, for instance in Japan, it is also preferable to be introduced by an independent third party rather than by a representative of one's company.

- *Provide references.* As we established earlier, members of strongly relationship-oriented cultures often look for references from trusted sources to assess the predictability of a prospective new partner. Having local contacts who can serve as references can be invaluable.

- *Bridge cultural gaps.* A sufficiently experienced local intermediary will be able to bridge at least some of the gap between the cultures, allowing business to be conducted with greater effectiveness.

- *Improve the communication.* Assuming the person has the necessary skills, your intermediary may serve as an interpreter and help by clarifying subtle messages, body language, and other forms of indirect communication. If you work with the individual in a continual basis, he or she will also greatly improve the ongoing communication with your counterparts and reduce the risk of misunderstandings.

- *Establish continual local representation.* The right intermediary may serve as a representative throughout the negotiation, which can be advantageous in certain cultures. Having a local sponsor or agent may even be a legal requirement, as is the case in countries such as Egypt and Saudi Arabia.

Choosing the right intermediary can be crucial. In strongly relationship-oriented cultures, the reputation and respect a foreign party will enjoy depend to a large degree on the standing its local representative has or is able to develop with the other party. Companies lacking the necessary contacts to identify a respected intermediary in a targeted country should contact a local embassy, a trade organization, a chamber of commerce, or a local legal or accounting firm that may be able to provide a list of potential candidates.

Since the person must have the right contacts and reputation, choosing a representative requires careful selection. In countries where relationships are critically important, such as China, Indonesia, or Japan, such a third-party contact will be equally cautious before agreeing to represent a foreign company. Introducing a party to his or her local contacts that turns out to be unreliable or not trustworthy could have huge consequences for the individual's own reputation and relationships.

While intermediaries are often helpful, using one is not always necessary, especially in many Western cultures. Making direct contact with the other side may be more appropriate, in which case one needs to determine how best to do so. An initial letter introducing the company, outlining its proposal, and requesting a meeting is often the most promising approach. In authoritarian and status-oriented cultures, the overall impression such a letter gives may become a decisive factor, making it important its appearance and wording are impeccable.

Since decision processes may be complex, involving various hierarchical levels and requiring consultations across large groups of people, it is often difficult to determine how much time to allow for a response. In the United States, it is not unusual to receive a call from the recipient of a contact letter on the day it is received. A delay of more than a few weeks generally signals that the other party is not interested in the proposed deal. In contrast, many Arabs, Asians, or Latin Americans may require at least several weeks before responding to such a letter. Inquiring about it during this time can be counterproductive since these counterparts may take this as a lack of patience and long-term focus.

Setting Up the Initial Meeting

Once another party has signaled interest in negotiating, a number of aspects must be considered before setting up an initial meeting:

- *Preparation time.* Expectations of how much time to allow for upfront preparation vary greatly. In some countries, a week's notice may suffice, while people in others may consider three or even four weeks as too short. Showing too great a sense of urgency may be taken as a lack of patience and can be counterproductive.

- *Choice of location.* From a cross-cultural perspective, it makes little difference whether a negotiation takes place at a home location, in a counterparts' country, or elsewhere.

The cultural distance between the parties, and thus the challenge to make the negotiation work, remains the same. Rules of etiquette may depend to a significant degree on the actual country where the negotiation takes place, though. Since unfamiliar settings tend to reduce people's comfort levels, it will generally be preferable to leverage the proverbial 'home advantage.' However, it is customary to let the party that has been contacted by the other choose the location.

- *Participants*. Which individuals need to attend an initial negotiation meeting depends to some degree on the cultural context. The core negotiation team (see also page 29) and any chosen intermediary, assuming that one is being used, will definitely be expected to attend. The Japanese, Mexicans, most Latin Americans, and others usually also expect a top executive on each side to attend the first meeting. This person will not be expected to attend subsequent meetings, though. Others, for instance the Chinese, Koreans, or Greeks, may expect continuous involvement of at least one senior executive throughout the negotiation. Members of a third cultural group, which includes Israel, the Nordics, Switzerland, the United States, and others, may not view the attendance of senior managers as essential. In any case, most counterparts will want to know upfront who will be attending the initial meeting, making it important to inform them in advance.

- *Agenda*. Setting an agenda ahead of the meeting is good practice. Doing so allows both parties to communicate upfront what they expect to cover in the meeting, giving them a chance to prepare and avoiding unwelcome surprises. If appropriate, one should propose an agenda and invite the other side to modify it as deemed necessary. The set agenda will not necessarily be followed, though, especially when meeting with members of highly polychronic cultures (see page 79).

The Critical First Meeting

As the old adage goes, "You will never get a second chance to make a first impression." When meeting foreign counterparts for the first time, chances are that the trust they are willing to place in a foreign visitor and the company he or she represent is much lower than if they were dealing with members of their own culture. The other party's representatives may initially remain cautious and reserved, sizing up the individual in order to determine whether the person is worthy of entertaining serious business discussions. First impressions become critically important at this point, as they are usually the basis for this decision.

Making matters even more challenging, people commonly tend to be less forgiving at first meetings than they may become down the road, when relationships have strengthened and trust has had a chance to develop. Comments or behaviors that may easily be forgiven in follow-on meetings could cause major issues at the critical initial one. It is vitally important to be 'on one's best behavior,' as viewed by the other party, when meeting for the first time. Below, we review aspects that require particular attention.

- *Timeliness*. Cultural context to a large degree determines punctuality expectations. For example, people in countries like Germany, Switzerland, or Japan expect visitors to be right on time, while Greeks, Turks, Mexicans, or Latin Americans might tolerate delays of 15 minutes or more without viewing them as significant. As a general rule, foreigners are usually expected to be punctual while locals may not be, and people of lower status are often made to wait while those of high status might be received immediately. It is best never to show signs of impatience or anger if made to wait at an initial meeting.

- *Personal appearance*. Though people's expectations will again depend on their cultural background, it is generally preferable to err on the conservative side when it comes to dress codes. If in doubt, better risk being slightly over-dressed rather than possibly appearing too casual. While body language and gestures also need to be adjusted to the specific culture, a few rules are universal. For instance, one should refrain from putting the hands on the hips, which is frequently interpreted as aggressive, or folding the arms, which many people interpret as defensive. Simi-larly, it is important not to stand too close to others or too far away, greet or talk to people with both hands in the pockets, or put the feet onto furniture. Any of these may insult some people.

- *Required protocol and formality.* The rules of what es-tablishes 'proper' behavior at business meetings can be amazingly complex. They often include numerous aspects that members of a cultural group deem important, such as naming conventions and the use of titles, how to intro-duce or greet people, how to hand out and receive busi-ness cards, the order in which individuals should enter a room, or where to be seated. Once the meeting itself has started, protocol rules may dictate who leads discussions, who gets to speak when, how much time to spend on in-troductions and small talk before focusing on business as-pects, which conversation topics to avoid, how to behave at the end of the meeting, and much more. While levels of formality vary considerably across cultures and some may generally be more forgiving than others, breaches of pro-tocol at best create awkward situations and at worst could bring negotiations to a premature end.

- *Humor.* Culture guides often point out that 'humor does not travel,' which seems to imply that it is best to avoid telling jokes or making humorous remarks when travel-ing abroad. While this is sound advice at least with a few cultures, it ignores the important role that humor plays in business in many countries. This is most pronounced in the Anglo-Saxon world, for instance in Australia, Canada, Ireland, the United Kingdom, or the United States, where showing a strong sense of humor is important as it helps 'break the ice,' allowing meeting participants to quickly focus on the business at hand. In contrast, using humor in business situations is not advisable in Japan and may be rare in Germany, the Netherlands, the Nordics, and several other countries. Since definitions of what constitutes a proper sense of humor vary much across cultures, it is vital to keep jokes light and friendly, staying away from remarks that might be perceived as cynical, sarcastic, or depreciative, even if made with the best of intentions.

- *Presentations.* While one might assume that presentation styles are mostly homogeneous in business around the world, members of different cultures may actually disagree over what constitutes a well-delivered presentation. It pays to study these differences, modifying materials and delivery of presentations accordingly, as this tends to help in making a favorable initial impression. Members of some cultures may expect formal presentations that include much background information about presenter and company, while others may look for lengthy technical explanations with many facts and details. Again others may not want to receive any formal presentation at the first meeting. One group may expect to be given room for extensive questioning and discussion, while another might consider interruptions rude. Providing copies of presentations and other handouts is always appreciated, especially when translated to local languages. However, whether people prefer these materials to look simple or to have strong visual appeal is again influenced by their respective cultural background.

Chapter 6: Negotiating and the Bargaining Exchange

Negotiation Attitudes

Behaviors and practices of negotiators around the world are strongly influenced by individual views of 'how to negotiate right.' Three principal attitudes are prevalent in domestic and international negotiations. They are mostly determined by the individuals' preferred levels of assertiveness and cooperation:

- *Cooperative.* These negotiators believe in the value of working together with their counterparts in order to solve what they see as a joint problem between the parties. Negotiators who truly embrace this attitude intend to collaborate with their counterparts for collective gain, looking to 'expand the pie' and share benefits equitably. This is commonly referred to as *win-win* negotiating. While individuals with this mindset might remain firm when required, they rarely see a need to be highly assertive. Members of several cultures, among them Anglo-Canadians, the Dutch, the French, Germans, Northern Europeans, the Japanese, Thais, and many Latin Americans, prefer such a cooperative approach. A related, though less effective way to reach consensus with a negotiation partner is to compromise. This requires both sides to make meaningful concessions in order to stimulate mutually acceptable solutions. Compromising is frequent in certain highly relationship-oriented cultures, for instance in Thailand, where it helps minimize conflict and disagreement. In contrast, compromising may be viewed as 'not trying hard enough' and is often disliked by people from countries such as the Netherlands, France, or Germany.

- *Competitive.* Most competitive negotiators consider negotiating a zero-sum game. In their view, one side's gain will need to equal the other side's loss. Accordingly, such individuals tend to be more assertive and less cooperative than those in the first group. Their strategies and tactics focus on winning concessions of greater value than they are prepared to give up in return. Haggling, which often creates competitive advantages with counterparts who are uncomfortable with repetitive back-and-forth exchanges, can be extensive with some individuals in this group. Though competitive negotiators may become emotionally involved in the process, most of them consider negotiating a game and expect their counterparts not to take any of their behaviors personally. Countries where negotiators tend to be competitive include Argentina, Brazil, China, India, Indonesia, Italy, Mexico, South Korea, Spain, Taiwan, the United States, and others.

- *Adversarial.* Adversarial negotiators are typically characterized by he lowest levels of cooperation and the highest degrees of assertiveness among the three groups. Rather than tracking and celebrating their own gains, many of them appear focused on the other party's losses. Instead of collaborating with their counterparts, adversarial negotiators frequently employ uncooperative and even aggressive approaches and behaviors. Others use passive-aggressive tactics, refusing to participate or fully engage in the negotiation exchange and pretending to be disinterested in their counterparts' offerings. These behaviors are nonconstructive and can make agreement between the parties very difficult to reach. Adversarial negotiators can be found anywhere in the world. They represent insignificant minorities in most countries. The small group of cultures where adversarial negotiating is more prevalent includes Russia and Ukraine. It is important to realize that this attitude does not necessarily reflect interpersonal animosity or hostile intentions. In fact, people who appear adversarial during the exchange may turn out to be friendly and sociable when away from the negotiation table.

While influenced by cultural context, negotiation attitudes mostly reflect individual preferences. Accordingly, none of the principal attitudes we describe is exclusive to any one culture, nor is any of them limited to a select group of countries. Highly adversarial negotiators may belong to cultures whose members generally prefer cooperative negotiating and vice versa. As a matter of fact, all three of these negotiation attitudes can be found anywhere around the world.

Conflicting attitudes can make it hard for negotiation parties to trust each other. However, it would be a mistake to assume that competitive or adversarial individuals invariably value relationships less than others do. It may seem counterintuitive that an apparently competitive or adversarial counterpart might belong to a strongly relationship-oriented society. However, members of such cultures might not necessarily consider these attitudes as inconsistent with their values. Some of them might view tough bargaining as a necessary precondition for lasting business engagements.

Bargaining Styles

Negotiation attitudes are mostly founded in individual negotiators' value systems. Such principal beliefs usually remain unchanged throughout negotiations. Nevertheless, experienced negotiators often employ multiple styles during the bargaining exchange, adjusting behaviors along the way as deemed necessary. The following bargaining styles are common:

- *Joint problem-solving.* This integrative bargaining style encourages the parties to work together constructively. Emphasizing a cooperative spirit, it relies on persuasion as the primary way to resolve disagreements. Though emotional pleas are not necessarily excluded, the use of rational arguments, supported by facts and figures, dominates the bargaining exchange between negotiators employing this style. Joint problem solving is common among cooperative negotiators and can be productive when dealing with highly competitive individuals as well. In contrast, adversarial negotiators rarely use this style.

- *Distributive bargaining.* If a party believes that the total value of the items being negotiated is fixed, it will likely adopt a distributive bargaining style. This commonly reflects competitive or adversarial negotiation attitudes. Such negotiators are rarely satisfied with both sides receiving equal benefits as a result of the bargaining exchange. Instead, many of them focus on winning as much as they possibly can. Common tactics indicating this style include bluffing and other deception tactics, threats and ultimatums, and general attempts to overpower or outsmart the other party.

- *Contingency bargaining.* A source of conflict and a frequent cause of disagreements between negotiating parties is that their assumptions about future trends and events may differ considerably. Contingency bargaining allows them to turn such a situation into a productive negotiation that focuses on credible scenarios. By introducing if-then clauses into the bargaining exchange, negotiators using this style can capture their own assumptions and those of their counterparts, stimulating constructive dialogues over how potential benefits will be distributed between the parties. Both cooperative or competitive negotiators may use this bargaining style. Since it requires a minimum level of collaboration between the parties, adversarial counterparts rarely adopt this style, though.

- *Debate.* Negotiators who prefer debating usually believe in the power of logical arguments, rhetoric, and intellectual capability. Debates tend to be less constructive than joint problem solving may be, where the parties focus on win-win results. Debates are normally stimulated by a negotiator's intent to persuade the other party to accept his or her position. Depending on the individual's objectivity and sense of fairness, either side might win such arguments. However, this bargaining style may lead to the parties 'digging in their heels' and getting stuck in non-constructive exchanges of positions. Debates are often initiated by strongly competitive or adversarial negotiators.

- *Non-directive discussion.* This explorative bargaining style aims to motivate negotiating parties to explore their assumptions and expectations. Since it is not necessarily designed to drive conclusions or to persuade others, this style is commonly employed in the information gathering phase and sometimes in the opening phase of the bargaining exchange. Negotiators using it are likely to switch to other styles when they believe that both sides are ready to work out their disagreements and identify acceptable settlement terms. Non-directive discussion requires cooperative attitudes on both sides of the negotiation table.

- *Relationship building.* This bargaining style can be valuable in strongly relationship-oriented cultures. It focuses on creating emotional bonds between the negotiating parties that are nurtured by mutual liking and trust. Negotiators using this style believe that trusting relationships are essential for successful business. They are often willing to compromise and make concessions as a way to indicate their commitment to a relationship. Though most popular among cooperative negotiators, this style is sometimes also employed by competitive ones.

Cultural factors significantly influence negotiators' choices of bargaining styles. Americans, Canadians, Dutch, Germans, Japanese, Northern Europeans, or Swiss people often prefer joint problem solving. The Chinese, Indians, Israelis, Russians, Taiwanese, Ukrainians, and many Latin Americans may favor distributive and contingency bargaining. Debating is a style frequently chosen by Australians, the French, French-Canadians, and Greeks. Building and leveraging relationships, while common across many cultures, may be particularly valued among Brazilians, Indonesians, Italians, Mexicans, Filipinos, Saudis, Spaniards, and Thais.

In any case, most negotiators will likely employ more than one of these styles during the bargaining exchange. For example, since smart negotiators pay attention to longer-term aspects of their business relationships, many of them combine competitive approaches with at least some cooperative elements. Generally competitive individuals may therefore compromise, make small concessions, or work with their counterparts in order to augment the mutual benefits of a proposed deal. This could reflect such individuals' realization that appearing competitive and unyielding throughout the exchange might cause their counterparts to become less cooperative. Nevertheless, such negotiators will likely continue to focus on coming out of the overall bargaining exchange ahead of their counterparts.

Another example for negotiators switching bargaining styles is that adversarial individuals often become more cooperative as the negotiation nears its end. Again, this aims to stimulate productive business relationships, even if the bargaining exchange itself was less constructive.

Being able to understand, recognize, and effectively deal with diverse negotiation attitudes and bargaining styles are vital skills for international negotiators. The most successful of them know how to control tone and atmosphere of the negotiation exchange independently of their counterparts' preferences. They do so by adjusting their own behaviors as appropriate, either by modifying attitudes and styles as appropriate or by employing negotiation techniques such as those described in Part II of this book, many of which serve to influence the other party's conduct and actions.

Bargaining Levers: Power, Information, and Time

The purpose of bargaining is to identify the terms under which the negotiating parties may reach agreement over a proposed deal. At its core, bargaining is a persuasion process designed to eliminate conflicting objectives, identify opportunities for mutual benefit, and find common ground between the parties. Persuasion mechanisms that might be employed during this exchange range from rational and logical reasoning to emotional, intuitive, and dogmatic appeals. While cultural preferences may drive certain preferences, people from all countries and cultures commonly employ any of these approaches.

In its most basic form, bargaining is the process that two negotiating parties use to identify an item's specific value that both of them consider attractive enough to agree with a transaction. For example, this could be the price for a product that one party intends to sell and the other intends to buy. Such an agreed value, or settling point, might lie anywhere within the settlement range shown in Figure 6.1.

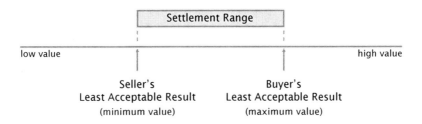

Figure 6.1 Settlement range.

The seller's and the buyer's respective Least Acceptable Result or LAR (see page 26) span the settlement range. Settlement might be impossible if the seller's LAR is higher than the buyer's LAR, that is, if the seller expects to receive more than the buyer is willing to give for the item under negotiation.

Being able to identify settlement ranges per Figure 6.1 is valuable in negotiations. However, real world business deals frequently show greater complexity and settling them may require reaching agreement over multiple items of tangible or intangible value. This could include identifying multiple settling points, accommodating both parties' assumptions about future events that could affect the negotiation outcome, and various other challenges.

The primary levers available to negotiators seeking to influence the other party's objectives, strategies, and decisions are power, information, and time. Skillful negotiators know how to advance their position and reduce the strength of their counterparts' position by utilizing all three of them:

- *Power.* Perceptions of power commonly influence most of the negotiating parties' decisions. How powerful a negotiator's position is perceived to be depends on a number of factors. Some of them, such as the size of the company represented and its available resources, are independent of the specific negotiation. Others may be situational. For example, if one side's BATNA is considerably more attractive than the other's, that party could strengthen its position by leveraging this knowledge as a pressure point during the bargaining exchange. Culture-specific factors may also have a significant impact on perceptions of power. They may be based on aspects such as status, rank, position, knowledge, experience, reputation, network and relationships, and more.

  Expectations of the distribution of power between buyers and sellers might also depend on the cultural context. Negotiators in countries such as Japan tend to attribute substantially more power to the buyer than to the seller, while members of egalitarian cultures, for instance the Dutch, may view both as equals.

  Smart negotiators realize that the concept of bargaining power is indeed subjective. They use this observation to their advantage, for instance by demonstrating attitudes, conveying expectations, and making demands that all signal a position of power. Such tactics might significantly improve a negotiator's position, even when dealing with counterparts whose bargaining power may seem superior. Effective countermeasures against such tactics include insisting on reciprocity in all exchanges of concessions, refusing to make repeat offers if an earlier one was rejected as 'not good enough,' and other behaviors that underline the equilibrium of power between the negotiating parties.

- *Information*. Any information that is available to a negotiating party might directly influence its strategies, tactics, and decisions. However, it is important to consider different categories. Information may be known, partially known, or unknown to either party. In addition, it might be real, presumed, or false. Information could be false because of misunderstandings between the parties, or because the party holding it was intentionally misled or even lied to. Such facets tend to complicate the exchange of information in international negotiations, which is often an intricate and convoluted process. In general, no strategy can be recommended universally for whether and when to share information. Negotiators facing such decisions must carefully consider a number of aspects. From a strategic standpoint, openly sharing all information about intentions, objectives, and goals is rarely in a negotiator's best interest. Not surprisingly, individuals taking this approach frequently find the results of negotiations to fall short of their expectations, especially when dealing with highly competitive counterparts. On the other hand, appearing to be hiding critical information is generally counterproductive. Members of several cultures, among them Americans, Australians, the British, Canadians, Indians, Northern Europeans, and others, view information sharing as a way to demonstrate good intentions and build trust. In contrast, most Russians, Turks, Ukrainians, and many others consider the same approach as naïve and foolish. These cultural preferences often correspond with preferred levels of uncertainty avoidance.

Key Concepts: High or Low Uncertainty Avoidance

Influential Dutch interculturalist Geert Hofstede identified a cultural characteristic he labeled **uncertainty avoidance**, defined as 'the extent to which members of a culture feel threatened by unknown or uncertain situations.'

People from cultures whose uncertainty avoidance is **high**, such as the French, the Japanese, South Koreans, Spaniards, and many Latin Americans, commonly prefer rules and structure over flexibility and 'creative chaos.' They may tolerate risk only if they are able to identify and analyze its components. Uncertain situations whose intrinsic risks remain unclear might cause high levels of anxiety. When negotiating, members of this group tend to dedicate substantial time and efforts to gathering and analyzing information about the other side. In addition, they often prefer contracts to be very detailed and explicit.

Conversely, people from **low** uncertainty avoidance cultures usually develop little anxiety over aspects which they cannot directly control. Often more curious and open to making changes than members of the first group are, they may be more willing to experiment and try out new ideas. This group of cultures includes Australia, Canada, India, Ireland, the United Kingdom, the United States, and others. Negotiators belonging to this group may consider extensive information gathering a waste of time, instead relying on their individual ability to navigate tricky situations and obtain information as needed.

Cultural preferences must be taken into account in all decisions about information sharing. In fact, failure to meet
others' expectations could cause irritation and jeopardize
relationships. In any case, certain practices are helpful regardless of the specific cultural context, as they commonly
make the negotiation process more effective. One of them
is to clarify technical and logistical requirements upfront,
since failing to do so may delay negotiations and force unnecessary concessions later on. Another useful practice is
to verify information through multiple sources whenever
possible. As we discussed in Chapter 2, doing so is always
advantageous. It can become crucial when dealing with
people from cultures where lies and deceits are common
when negotiating. Lastly, another good practice is to dis-
close alternative goals as a way to break up negotiation
impasses if required.

- *Time.* Time constraints frequently create pressure in negotiations. There are two effective ways for negotiators to
impose such time pressure and use it to their advantage.
One is to leverage real or artificial deadlines, for instance
by stating that a proposed deal will only be feasible if accepted by a certain date or time. By using this approach,
negotiators may be able to instill fear in their counterparts
that the deal might be off unless it is accepted as proposed.
This could make the other party more conciliatory. However, this method of leveraging time tends to make negotiations less constructive, since it is often perceived as
highly adversarial. It therefore requires careful planning
and execution to avoid adversely impacting relationships
between the parties.

  More promising, especially when dealing with people
from fast-paced cultures where 'time is money,' such as
the United States or Canada, is an alternate method of creating time pressure. It relies on using others' self-imposed
deadlines or impatience against them and is frequently
practiced by members of many cultures, among them most

Asians, Latin Americans, and Southern Europeans. Upon learning that a counterpart is working against a deadline, such as a scheduled departure date or a time commitment made to someone else, members of these cultures may stall the bargaining exchange until shortly before this deadline, knowing that the other individual will likely become more inclined to make concessions in order to successfully close the deal in the remaining time. If no such deadline exists, procrastinating and generally slowing down the bargaining exchange may be effective as well, since doing so also creates a perceived incentive for the other party to make concessions in order to 'get things going again.' Because of such psychological pressure effects, time is commonly a more valuable lever for the negotiating party that is the most patient and persistent. Negotiators around the world use such tactics to offset differences in power or available information between the negotiating parties.

Making Offers and Concessions

When preparing to bargain, three highly interdependent aspects of concession making require careful consideration: pattern (number of bargaining rounds), timing (when to make offers and counteroffers), and magnitude (how small or large each concession should be). These decisions can be critical for the negotiation outcome.

Opening offers represent the first major challenge. They require implicit or explicit decisions between the parties as to which side will start the exchange. People from many cultures commonly expect the seller to open the bargaining. There may be reasons to ignore this practice, but in general, the importance of 'who goes first' tends to be overrated. Negotiators who are unsure of an item's real value usually have the option to start with an extreme opening offer, which frequently helps to obtain clues about the item's true value from the other party. As a matter of fact, research results suggest that negotiators starting with extreme openings on average achieve higher settlements than those making seemingly more realistic opening offers.

The message sent through the opening offer must be viewed as constructive by the other party and therefore requires considering culture-specific expectations. In the United States, such expectations may be that the offer is clear and positive, creates interest, stresses mutual benefits, and implies flexibility. Extreme opening offers only meet these expectations if not outrageously mismatched with the perceived value of the item or items being negotiated. In contrast, expectations in Arab countries may include that the opening offer leaves considerable room for haggling, stimulates negotiators' creativity, and signals interest in engaging in extensive bargaining exchanges with the other party.

Once an opening offer has been put on the table, a process of exchanging offers and counteroffers follows. The structure of this process is usually unpredictable. However, many aspects are influenced by cultural preferences. Researchers Donald Hendon and Rebecca Angeles Hendon conducted an interesting study regarding the timing and pattern of concession making. They presented negotiators from several countries with different patterns of sizing and timing concessions over subsequent bargaining rounds. The following table shows a few patterns used by the researchers and lists the strategy behind each of them:

	Round				
Pattern	One	Two	Three	Four	Strategy
A	25	25	25	25	equivalent concessions
B	100	-	-	-	immediate submission
C	-	-	-	100	tough bargaining
D	10	20	30	40	protracted concessions
E	40	30	20	10	diminishing concessions

Members of several cultures were asked to identify the patterns they liked best and those they disliked the most. The results suggest strong cultural bias. While most participants neither liked nor disliked equivalent concessions (pattern A) and almost everyone disliked immediate submission (B), the other patterns triggered responses which depended significantly on the respondents' cultural background.

Tough bargaining (C) was generally favored by negotiators from competitive cultures, such as Americans and Brazilians. Israelis, Russians, or Ukrainians, none of whom were included in the study, might show similar preferences. In strongly harmony-oriented Asian cultures such as Indonesia or Malaysia, this pattern is generally not favored and may even be viewed as adversarial.

The strategy to make protracted concessions (D) generally creates incentives for persistent counterparts willing to spend considerable time negotiating. This pattern is favored by many Asians, for instance the Hong Kong Chinese, Filipinos, Indians, Indonesians, or Singaporeans, as well as others not included in the study, such as the Chinese. While many Americans also like this approach, they tend to increase concessions faster and will likely expect to go through fewer rounds of bargaining than Asians may. In cultures where bargaining is generally disliked, protracted concessions may be considered as uncooperative.

Diminishing concessions (E) are commonly preferred by Australians, Canadians, the Taiwanese, Thais, or Northern Europeans. This pattern is often well liked in cultures whose members expect the bargaining exchange to be short and mostly free of haggling. Around the world, making diminishing concessions is an acceptable strategy.

Patterns of individual concession making become even more complicated in negotiations that extend over multiple items. While a discussion of specific strategies would take us beyond the scope of this book, we should at least introduce one relevant characteristic that becomes important in this type of negotiations: the concept of *polychronicity*.

Key Concepts: Polychronic versus Monochronic Cultures

People who prefer ***monochronic*** work styles are used to pursuing actions and goals in a systematic fashion. Most of them tend to be punctual, value order and predictability, frequently use checklists, follow preset meeting agendas, and generally dislike interruptions or digressions. When negotiating, they often work their way down sequential lists of objectives, bargaining for each item separately. They may be unwilling to revisit aspects that had already been agreed upon. Monochronic people generally prefer to capture information in writing and may insist that written protocols and other papers be used to document interim agreements.

In contrast, people who prefer ***polychronic*** work styles are used to pursuing multiple actions and goals in parallel. They pay less attention to punctuality, value flexibility and spontaneity, enjoy changing concepts, ignore preset meeting agendas, and generally dislike routine work and bureaucracy. People with this preference often keep a holistic view of the overall negotiation process. They may jump back and forth between topics rather than addressing them in sequential order. In addition, they generally prefer to convey information orally so they can get immediate feedback or make changes on the fly.

Negotiators whose cultural and personal preferences are on opposite ends of this spectrum may struggle to tolerate the resulting differences. Members of strongly monochronic cultures, such as Americans, the British, Canadians, Germans, Northern Europeans, and the Swiss, tend to consider polychronic styles as confusing, irritating, and even annoying. In turn, members of strongly polychronic cultures, for example Brazilians, the Chinese, Egyptians, the French, Indians, Mexicans, Russians, Spaniards, and Venezuelans, often consider monochronic behaviors as closed-minded and overly restrictive. Both sides may view their own preferred styles as more effective. In any case, it is vital not to show irritation or anger when encountering behavior that conflicts with personal preferences.

Cultural influences are only one of the factors that determine such preferences. Although most cultures generally encourage one or the other, members of generally polychronic societies may prefer monochronic styles and vice versa.

Myths About Bargaining

As we have shown, bargaining exchanges are commonly shaped by a complex array of style preferences and strategic variants. That notwithstanding, a number of alleged 'truths' about bargaining are often brought up as guidance for inexperienced negotiators. Upon closer inspection, most such guidelines turn out to be culture-specific rather than universally applicable. Let us take a look at three popular myths:

- *"Tough wins."* This statement implies that negotiators who 'play hardball' and whose attitudes are generally highly competitive or adversarial have a greater chance of coming out ahead in negotiations. In actuality, this is rarely the case. Since humans commonly tend to 'fight fire with fire,' negotiations that are led in this spirit often escalate unnecessarily. In particular, negotiators in many strongly relationship-oriented cultures are less likely to cooperate with such tough negotiators. Their concessions during bargaining exchanges may therefore become smaller and less valuable, which is why tough negotiators rarely get the best deals possible.

   In contrast, a more universally valid statement is that 'firm wins.' Remaining firm at critical points during the negotiation exchange is respected by members of most cultures as long as the individual doing so demonstrates flexibility in other areas. Unlike being tough, firmness in select areas may be combined with highly collaborative behaviors in others, which can be a winning negotiation strategy.

- *"Winning makes people happy."* Although competitive individuals may strongly believe in its validity, this statement is not universally accepted either. People in many cultures tend to take an individual's passion for winning as indication of a win-lose mindset that is likely to leave one party with a less desirable outcome than the other. Highly cooperative negotiators, as well as members of strongly relationship-oriented cultures, are particularly likely to reject this attitude. Some in the latter group might even argue that it can be advantageous to be the 'loser' in a negotiation if making significant concessions paves the road to productive long-term business relationships. Even though the underlying intentions may be right, it is therefore generally not advisable to express a strong passion for winning when negotiating across cultures.

- *"It is important to keep the highest aspirations."* This piece of advice, which can be found in books about effective negotiation strategies, represents another popular myth. Keeping high aspirations throughout the negotiation process is unquestionably a sound strategy. Doing so encourages negotiators to explore ways to maximize the benefits of the business deal at hand, which often adds value for both parties. However, keeping the highest aspirations implies that a negotiator must focus on achieving the best possible outcome of the bargaining exchange rather than remaining cooperative and flexible. This may again violate the spirit of give-and-take that people in many cultures expect from their counterparts and could make the overall process less productive.

Decision Making

Key Concepts: Individualistic versus Group-Oriented Cultures

Members of strongly *individualistic cultures* value each person's preferences and desires. In these societies, individual decision making is generally encouraged and each individual may be held responsible for his or her own mistakes. The authority to make decisions either resides with top executives or it is delegated to lower levels in the organization. Those in charge do not necessarily have to consult with others before making decisions. Because of this, decision making can be quick. Consensus decision making is rare and is often considered too slow and ineffective by people in this category, which includes Americans, Australians, Canadians, the Dutch, Scandinavians, and others.

In strongly *group-oriented cultures*, individual preferences are generally considered less important than having a sense of belonging to the group, conforming to its norms, and maintaining harmony among its members. Such a group might be an individual's extended family, an organization, a social group, or the society as a whole. In group-oriented cultures, decision making usually requires involving everyone who may be affected. It could even require reaching consensus among all of the group's members. Since this can be very time consuming, decision making is often slow in such a cultural environment. The group as a whole is responsible for mistakes, even if individual members made them. Top executives supervise and coordinate the decision process. While their inputs often carry significant weight, they rarely act as sole decision makers. Most Asian cultures are strongly group-oriented, among them China, India, Indonesia, Japan, Malaysia, the Philippines, and Taiwan. Mexicans and most Latin Americans are also generally group-oriented, as are Greeks, the Portuguese, Turks, and numerous others.

Concepts of how decisions are made and who is involved in the process vary across organizations and cultures. Figure 6.2 explores possible structures of the negotiation exchange, assuming that decisions on the buyer's side are made by a single individual.

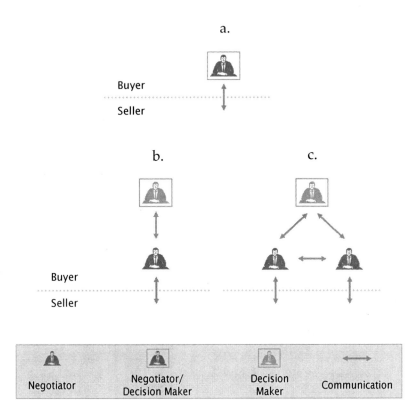

Figure 6.2 Individual decision making in negotiations.

- *Individual decision making - structure a.* Only one negotiator representing the buyer communicates with the seller.
  Though he or she may consult with others, this negotiator
  is the ultimate decision maker and does not require others'
  approval. In order to reach agreement, the seller needs to
  win the decision maker's support.

- *Individual decision making - structure b.* Only one negotiator representing the buyer communicates with the seller.
  However, the person acts as an intermediary. Decisions on
  the buyer's side are made by another individual, typically
  someone higher up in the hierarchy, who usually does not
  attend negotiation meetings. In order to reach agreement,
  the seller needs to get access to and win the support of the
  decision maker. Alternatively, the seller could try to win
  the intermediary's support, relying on that person's ability
  to influence the decision maker.

- *Individual decision making - structure c.* Several negotiators representing the buyer communicate with the seller,
  acting as intermediaries. Decisions on the buyer's side are
  made by another individual, typically someone higher up
  in the hierarchy, who usually does not attend negotiation
  meetings. In order to reach agreement, the seller needs to
  get access to and win the support of the decision maker.
  Alternatively, the seller could try to win the support of all
  or most of the intermediaries, relying on their ability to
  influence the decision maker.

All of these structures of individual decision making are
predominantly found in individualistic cultures. The differences between them reflect two preferences: whether the
negotiation meetings are attended by a single individual or
by a group representing the buyer, and whether the decision
maker is or is not directly involved in meetings and negotiation exchanges. If the decision maker does not attend meetings (structures b. or c.), this usually indicates either that the

deal being negotiated is not viewed as important or that the status of the seller's most senior representative is perceived to be lower than that of the decision maker on the buyer's side. The choice of using more than one negotiator, as illustrated by structure c., may be influenced by a number of factors, which include individual participants' competencies and how the seller's team is composed, as well as corporate practices, legal aspects, and cultural orientations.

From the seller's perspective, the common denominator of the structures we have discussed so far is that the buyer's decisions are made by only one individual. While intermediaries might influence decisions to some degree, reaching agreement ultimately requires winning the support of the key person. In contrast, Figure 6.3 illustrates possible group decision-making structures, which often require more complex persuasion strategies.

- *Group decision making - structure a.* Only one negotiator representing the buyer communicates with the seller, acting as an intermediary. The person also participates in making decisions. Others who usually do not attend negotiation meetings are also involved in the decision making process. Decisions might require reaching consensus among all involved or obtaining final approval by the most senior person. In order to reach agreement, the seller needs to win the support of most or all decision makers. Winning only the intermediary's support and relying on that person's ability to influence the other decision makers may not be a sufficient basis for reaching agreement.

- *Group decision making - structure b.* Two or more negotiators representing the buyer communicate with the seller. They are involved in the decision making process, as are others who usually do not attend negotiation meetings. Decisions might require reaching consensus among all involved or obtaining final approval by the most senior person. In order to reach agreement, the seller needs to win the support of most or all of the decision makers, including those absent from meetings. Alternatively, the seller could try to win the support of those attending the negotiation meetings, relying on their ability to influence the absent decision makers.

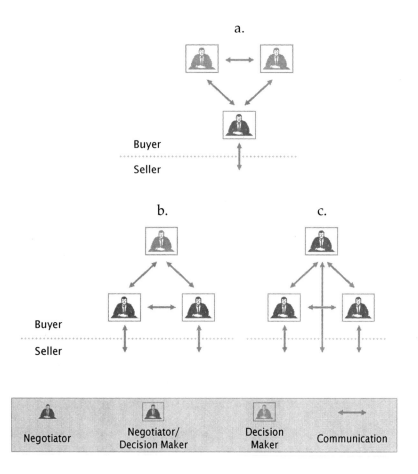

Figure 6.3 Group decision making in negotiations.

- *Group decision making - structure c.* Two or more negotiators representing the buyer communicate with the
  seller and jointly make decisions. Decision making might
  require reaching consensus among all involved. The representatives do not need to involve others when making
  decisions. In order to reach agreement, the seller needs to
  win the support of all or most of the decision makers. Winning only the support of the highest ranking person may
  not be a sufficient basis for reaching agreement.

Companies and organizations in group-oriented cultures
commonly employ one of the decision making structures per
Figure 6.3 when negotiating. Interactions that reflect structures a. or b. may indicate either that the deal being negotiated is not viewed as important or that the status of the seller's
most senior representative is perceived to be lower than that
of the highest ranking person on the buyer's side. The use of
structure a. is rare, since most organizations in these cultures
prefer to be represented by more than one individual.

We should emphasize that group decision making does not
necessarily requires consensus. In cultures that are either
highly egalitarian or strongly focused on preserving group
harmony, establishing consensus among all team members
may be the expected norm. In many other group-oriented
cultures, though, decision making may only require that everyone is given a chance to express his or her opinion before
final decisions are made.

Group-oriented decision making does not mean that every
voice will carry equal weight. On the other hand, it can be
dangerous to rely solely on the support of one or a few key
influencers in a group, no matter how powerful they may
appear to be within its hierarchy. A more promising strategy
when dealing with such cultures is to invest the time and
energy to build relationships with all or most of the group's
members, especially those who may be key influencers, and
with the final decision maker, assuming such a role exists.

Decision making structures as presented in Figures 6.2 and 6.3 are obviously influenced by cultural preferences for individualism or group orientation, as well as those for egalitarianism or authoritarianism. A third culture-specific factor also warrants careful consideration in this context. It describes the propensity of members of a given culture to follow universalistic principles or to consider situational aspects when making decisions.

Key Concepts: Universalistic versus Particularistic Cultures

Members of strongly **universalistic cultures** prefer to follow established rules and practices when making decisions. For them, empirical evidence and other objective facts often weigh more strongly than personal feelings and experiences do. They dislike making exceptions, even if several facts speak in favor. In addition, they value contracts and usually expect them to be kept without exception. When confronted with new situations, people sharing this preference may concentrate on aspects of universal validity rather than looking for unique findings and observations. Typical representatives of this group of cultures are Americans, Australians, the British, Canadians, the Dutch, Germans, Northern Europeans, the Swiss, and others.

In strongly **particularistic cultures**, people making decisions will focus most of their attention onto the specific aspects of a situation and the people involved in it. Doubtful of absolute truths and convinced that the world around them is in constant motion, many of them are mistrustful of universal rules and norms. Most members of this group are highly relationship-oriented. They tend to consider legal contracts mere formalities, expecting partners to remain flexible and relying on the strength of relationships to ensure that agreements are kept. The group of particularistic cultures includes most Asian and Arab ones, as well as France, Greece, Italy, Mexico, Russia, Spain, Turkey, all of Latin America, and many other countries.

Successfully influencing decisions requires understanding and properly dealing with people's preferences. With members of universalistic cultures, it can be highly beneficial to identify established precedents which they might be able to follow, especially if a proposed deal requires them to consider unusual circumstances. In contrast, asking them to make a decision 'as a personal favor' may make these individuals suspicious and might be counterproductive. When dealing with people from particularistic cultures, on the other hand, it is often more advantageous to appeal to their intuition and to emphasize how a proposed deal will help strengthen relationships between the negotiating parties.

Chapter 7: Agreement, Closure, and Execution

Reaching Agreement

Key Concepts: Tentative Agreement – Agreement – Contract

Words which may seem clear within the framework of one country's cultural and legal context sometimes take on a different meaning ina different one. For example, the term *agreement* may be understood as final and dependable consent in one culture, while members of another culture may take it to mean little more than general intentions. Similarly, while people in one country may consider contracts irrevocable documents that must be followed to the letter, others may view them as summaries of past agreements that remain subject to change. Throughout this book, we take these terms to mean the following:

Tentative agreement is an intention shared by both sides to accept a negotiated condition in the future if certain expectations are met, for instance that the parties will reach consensus over items that are subject to further bargaining, that a proposed agreement will find the consent of decision makers who are not at the negotiation table, or that yet-to-be-verified information will prove correct. The negotiating parties usually acknowledge implicitly or explicitly that final agreement is contingent upon these and other factors. Tentative agreements may exist in oral form or in writing.

Agreement (sometimes referred to as *final agreement*) requires both parties to confirm their acceptance of a negotiated set of conditions with the intention to carry out all of the resulting obligations. Agreements can be closed orally or in writing. Depending on a country's legal system, agreements may or may not be legally binding.

> **Contract** is a written document that confirms closure of an agreement between negotiating parties. Contracts commonly spell out all negotiated terms and conditions, as well as resulting obligations for both parties. Most such documents include provisions for cases such as modification, termination, or breach of contract. Contracts normally become binding when both parties accepted them through their signatures.

The process negotiators prefer to use in order to reach agreement may depend on their cultural background. Members of monochronic cultures, which includes Americans, Canadians, Germans, people from the Nordics, or the Swiss, tend to rely on iterative approaches. Since their propensity is commonly to work down lists of objectives in sequential order, bargaining for each item separately, they may seek to establish tentative agreement after each round. This is often documented through written protocols or meeting summaries. At major milestones, negotiators with this preference may request that tentative agreement be confirmed by the parties signing written documents such as Memorandums of Understanding (MoA) or Letters of Intent (LoI). These papers may have legal implications that need to be assessed. However, their primary role is usually to confirm mutual understanding and to reaffirm both parties' commitment to resolve remaining issues and disagreements. The dependability of tentative agreements, whether oral or in writing, might vary considerably across cultures.

Since members of polychronic cultures, for example the French, most Latin Americans, or Arabs from the Middle East, generally prefer a holistic approach that considers all aspects that are required in order to reach agreement, they are less inclined to work down itemized lists one by one. Accordingly, they may be reluctant to accept tentative agreements. When dealing with such negotiators, one should diligently track concessions on both sides as well as areas where consensus seems possible. However, it is best to remain open to revisiting individual aspects if requested by the other side.

Indicators that agreement is within reach and that a counterpart may be ready to close a deal depend to some degree on his or her cultural context. In countries where people enjoy bargaining and haggling, such as most Arab countries, Indonesia, Nigeria, Pakistan, the Philippines, or Turkey, a telling sign is often that subsequent concessions are getting smaller. With other negotiators, there could be a general shift in the focus of attention. For instance, when polychronic negotiators start addressing specific issues and details, this often indicates that they are ready to close. This applies especially to members of strongly relationship-oriented cultures, among them many Chinese, Egyptians, Greeks, Indonesians, Malaysians, or Singaporeans, but also to people from other polychronic cultures, for instance the French. In contrast, Americans, Germans, and others belonging to monochronic and task-oriented cultures may start to focus on bigger-picture aspects. Again, this is often a sign that they are ready to close the agreement. Several techniques to test and establish agreement are discussed in Part II of this book.

In previous chapters, we repeatedly mentioned the importance of patience and persistence for international negotiators. These qualities are imperative when trying to reach agreement and closure. In the eyes of many people around the world, impatience indicates a lack of commitment to and respect for the business relationship, a lack of personal discipline, or both. Either interpretation is prone to reduce a counterpart's comfort level and may complicate or delay closure.

Once agreement has been reached, symbolic acts commonly confirm the parties' intentions to honor it. This usually precedes the formal contract signature. One such act is the exchange of handshakes between the lead negotiators or between team members on both sides. Some Asians, for example the Japanese, usually confirm the mutual agreement by both parties stating precisely what it is they agree with. Written documents may serve for the same purpose and might be used in many cultures. In general, capturing agreements in writing is always recommended in international business, since this reduces the risk of communication failure and misunderstandings. It is usually not necessary –and sometimes unwise– to insist that such documents be signed. Doing so may be interpreted as a lack of trust. The same could be true if a negotiator demanded that the write-up include all details of the agreement. Some counterparts may be more comfortable with keeping this document high-level, capturing only the essential spirit of the agreement between the parties.

Closure: The Role of Contracts

Structure and content of contracts are commonly driven by company policies and practices, legal considerations, third-party requirements, and other factors. In addition, cultural preferences tend to have a significant influence on how businesspeople view the importance of a contract and how much detail they expect to be included. Four main categories can be identified:

- *Detailed contracts are preferred; they are viewed as important.* Cultures sharing this preference include Austria, Canada, Germany, the Netherlands, the Nordic countries, Switzerland, the United Kingdom, and the United States. Australians, the French, Hong Kong Chinese, and Israelis also often fall into this category, though they may be less obsessed over contractual details than others may. Generally, people in this group tend to view contracts as critical instruments, capturing all of the partners' resulting obligations, including provisions for many eventualities, and relying on legal enforcement if necessary to ensure that agreements be kept. Some of them may actually not believe that final agreement has been reached until the final version of the contract has been accepted by both parties. They might actually use the process of creating the contract as an opportunity to continue or re-open the bargaining exchange.

- *Detailed contracts are preferred; they are viewed as a formality.* A diverse group of cultures falls into this category, including Ireland, Italy, most Latin American countries, Pakistan, Philippines, Portugal, Singapore, South Korea, Spain, and others. Usually more strongly relationship-oriented than those in the first category, members of this group see contracts primarily as a communication tool. By capturing much detail, they verify both parties' understanding of the agreement. Nevertheless, they prefer to rely more on the relationship itself than on the disciplinary nature of the contract. The time it may take to complete a contract could be substantial in these cultures, though.

- *High-level contracts are preferred; they are viewed as important.* Cultures in this group, which includes India, Russia, South Africa, and Ukraine, tend to combine Western influences emphasizing the importance of written contracts with a relationship orientation that motivates people to focus on the essential aspects of the agreement rather than spelling out many details. Writing up a contract may still be time consuming in these countries as much attention may be given to its language and content.

- *High-level contracts are preferred; they are viewed as a formality.* This category includes countries such as China, Egypt, Greece, Indonesia, Malaysia, Mexico, Saudi Arabia, Taiwan, and Thailand. Since their cultures emphasize the importance of relationships, members of this group tend to pay little attention to contractual aspects unless legal circumstances force them to. Nevertheless, the final step of both parties formally signing the document may be highly ceremonial and is often celebrated with banquets and other events. The exchange of gifts is also common on these occasions. All of these practices commonly serve to strengthen relationships between the partners.

Note that a few cultures do not clearly fall into any of the above categories. For instance, while contracts are often a mere formality in underdeveloped countries like Nigeria, a wide range of styles may be found, reaching from those oriented at a high level to others which are very detailed. This sometimes reflects historic influences by foreign nations and individual companies.

Another exception is Japan: historically, this society had no use or need for contracts, since its strict system of honor and public enforcement provided the necessary checks and balances between business partners. Today, many Japanese still dislike closing written contracts, instead relying on written protocols and the strength of relationships.

Execution: After the Contract Has Been Signed

When conducting international business, it is crucial to recognize that negotiations do not end with the signing of the contract. Before the parties enter into the execution phase of a negotiation, three aspects require particular consideration:

- *Importance of commitments and deadlines.* What international partners view as commitments is not necessarily restricted to aspects that are clearly spelled out in contracts. Members of some cultures may also expect oral commitments or those captured in written exchanges and protocols to be dependable. The degree to which they expect such commitments to be met might vary considerably across cultures. While some partners may reject even a day's delay or a minor variation from an asserted product characteristic as unacceptable, others might remain casual about much more significant deviations. This emphasizes the importance of discussing and documenting such expectations during the closure phase of the negotiation, which can be extremely helpful should disagreements surface over such aspects later on.

- *Contract modifications and post-contract negotiation.* Around the world, business contracts commonly state that modifications require the consent of all contract partners. Such requests may actually lead to tensions between the parties. International partners, in particular members of strongly relationship-oriented cultures, often expect their counterparts to remain flexible should conditions change. This includes agreeing to modified contract terms and showing willingness to ignore some of them if necessary. Rejecting such requests could be detrimental to the relationship and tends to affect the other party's contract compliance. Moreover, businesspeople from China, South Korea, and several other countries frequently request contract changes, sometimes already a few weeks after the contract signing ceremony. Unlike Westerners, who often view contracts as continually binding documents designed to stand the test of time, members of these cultures tend to take them merely as reflections of both parties' intentions at the time they were signed. To them, the emergence of new facts or circumstances justifies requests to revisit aspects of the contract. When negotiating with such counterparts, it is therefore wise to consider the possibility of having to make additional concessions down the road.

- *Enforceability.* Few areas hold greater potential for culture clash than the legal enforcement of agreements and contracts. In countries with highly developed legal systems, business partners commonly rely on the framework they provide as a force to stimulate contract fulfillment. Whether or not contract partners are likely to take legal action against a counterpart who failed to fulfill contractual obligations often depends on the role relationships play in the country. For example, while litigation is a likely action in the United States or Canada in such a case, this option is rarely a choice in Japan. The Japanese and members of most other strongly relationship-oriented cultures prefer to resolve such issues through mediation or continued negotiation as required to restore full cooperation between the partners. In countries whose legal systems are less developed, the strength of relationships frequently determines whether and to what extent agreements are fulfilled. Regardless of the legal context, keeping in touch on a regular basis and continually nurturing close ties with partners who strongly focus on relationships is a powerful way to ensure that they will keep their commitments. Even in countries where legal systems are dependable, Alternative Dispute Resolution (ADR) through trained mediators is usually preferable over litigation. This approach often clears the path to maintaining or restoring business relationships.

Chapter 8: Why International Negotiations Fail

Attitudes

Below, we list a number of symptoms that commonly indicate company practices that may not be well tuned to the requirements of global business. These signs may be warning of an increased possibility of failing international negotiations and should therefore raise red flags for company management and negotiators alike. Some of the underlying issues may not necessarily be of consequence to the negotiation exchange itself. However, serious issues might surface once the negotiating parties have entered into the execution phase of an agreement between them.

- The company's leaders are unable to clearly communicate its reasons for seeking an international partner.

- Company management considers language, time zone differences, or trade laws and other legal implications the biggest obstacles to doing business globally.

- The company considers international business as secondary to its domestic goals and objectives.

- Executives believe that foreign business is little more than an extension of domestic business.

- Middle management feels that international partners cannot be trusted.

- Employees question the validity of the company going international, fearing job losses and reduced influence.

- Previous international business deals have fallen apart for reasons that are unclear, since they were not properly analyzed.

- International engagements are motivated by coincidences ("We happened to know a capable guy over there, so we established our office in Paris.") or based on subjective criteria ("Our boss likes visiting Japan, which is why we are looking for a partner there.")

Normally, these issues alone do not cause international deals to fail. However, they signal troublesome underlying attitudes that likely determine values, practices, and behaviors of negotiators directly involved in international deal making and others expected to support and execute the resulting agreements. If these individuals' attitudes clash with the required collaborative spirit, the chances of the cooperation being productive and sustainable will at best be slim.

A Few Case Studies

Case A: Americans in China

Attracted by the growing prosperity of the emerging middle class in China, Orange Corp., a successful U.S. brand of electronic entertainment products, decided to build a stronger presence in the country's consumer markets. The American team identified Chinese retail company Lucky Sun as a potential partner who appears to have the wherewithal required to support Orange's successful market entry.

Negotiations were intense and fierce. Committed to moving forward as quickly as possible, Orange Corp. wasted little time in preliminaries and kept a high sense of urgency throughout the negotiation. Realizing the market potential of Orange's products, Lucky Sun went along and, while negotiating fiercely, demonstrated its willingness to reach a mutually acceptable agreement. Because of the rapid pace, relationships between both sides remained somewhat perfunctory, which few among Orange's senior managers considered an issue.

After much back-and-forth bargaining, the parties put together a detailed contract and eventually signed it in a festive ceremony. Lucky Sun immediately started developing a marketing campaign designed to stimulate sales of Orange's products. However, a week before the planned release date of the campaign, Lucky Sun contacted Orange to request a higher retail margin than the contract between the companies provided for. Its management argued that the Chinese government had just released new regulations that would cause the cost of product returns, and thus Lucky Star's handling cost, to increase considerably. The contract included no provisions for such a case.

Orange's management immediately rejected the request. The company sent a corporate lawyer to China with the charter to remind Lucky Sun that the existing contract spelled out that margins would not be renegotiated during the first three years of the agreement. Lucky Sun appealed to Orange's chief executive, only to receive a harsh statement emphasizing that the partnership required both sides to honor their contractual agreements and adding that Orange considered the case closed.

A few days later, Lucky Sun decided to stop the marketing campaign. In fact, the retailer subsequently started actively promoting a competing South Korean brand, which eventually led to Orange filing a Civil Enforcement lawsuit against Lucky Sun in a local Chinese court. Today, more than three years after the original contract was signed, this lawsuit is still pending. After extensive market research and negotiations, Orange managed to sign up another retailer to support its Chinese market entry. It is paying that retailer a higher margin than it would have paid Lucky Sun.

This case presents a typical example of misaligned expectations and a lack of cross-cultural understanding on both sides. The American side failed to recognize the importance of relationship building and the different views the partners held of the role of contracts. The Chinese side may have failed to understand the pending changes in regulations. It also did not recognize that the American company expected its contract to be honored to the letter, not only in spirit. Accordingly, the Americans cried foul when the Chinese 'violated' the contract by requesting better terms after signature, while the Chinese took the apparent unwillingness to be flexible as indication that the Americans had no intentions to collaborate as trustworthy business partners. Had both parties understood each other's cultural framework better, they might have been able to identify a mutually acceptable solution to the situation.

Case B: Canadians in Turkey

Looking to expand its international sales, Canadian chemical company Chemron identified a sizable Turkish industrial conglomerate as a potential customer for industrial chemicals. Erkan Industries, the Turkish firm, was known to be dissatisfied with its current supplier.

Realizing the importance of relationship building and establishing local contacts, Chemron followed a suggestion by the Canadian chamber of commerce to hire a local representative in Turkey. Recruiting this individual indeed proved valuable, since he quickly managed to make contact with a senior manager at one of Erkan's numerous subsidiaries. After two meetings and a pleasant business dinner, relationships seemed to develop well between Chemron's negotiators and that manager. He promised to get the Canadians in touch with a key influencer within Erkan's extensive corporate hierarchy. Indeed, meeting with that executive seemed promising since he displayed sincere interest in Chemron's capabilities. In addition, he put its representatives in touch with another senior Erkan executive whose support he felt would be crucial.

Although the overall progress was slower than expected, Chemron was optimistic at becoming the Turkish company's primary vendor. After further efforts to strengthen relationships, its representatives submitted a formal offer outlining why Chemron was the right choice for Erkan and how it would be able to meet all of the customer's needs. This offer received much attention from Erkan's managers, some of whom pulled in others at the company who were asked to meet with the Canadians in order to further review and discuss the offer.

A week later, the Canadian team learned to its great surprise that Erkan had just awarded a large contract for the procurement of industrial chemicals to one of Chemron's competitors. This move would effectively shut out the Canadian company from most of the potential business with this customer. Neither its own contacts at Erkan nor the hired Turkish representative had given Chemron any indication that the negotiation was not going well.

In this case, most of the blame goes to the Canadian negotiators. Although they recognized cultural differences and tried to adjust to them, for instance by making efforts to build and strengthen relationships, they apparently failed to realize that they were in fact dealing with the wrong contacts. It is likely that the representatives of the Turkish company they were dealing with neither had the authority to make the required procurement decisions nor had any significant influence in the decision process. In cultures where personal pride is very important, such facts may not necessarily be revealed. The Turks may have dedicated their time because they were interested in exploring other opportunities or simply in learning more about the other party in general. This is not an unusual experience when doing business in Turkey, making it vital to identify the true decision makers before starting to negotiate with companies in the country. The local representative the Canadians had selected obviously lacked the insight and contacts required to recognize the situation.

Case C: Germans in Mexico

German carmaker ALV determined that its most promising option to establish a stronger presence in the important North American auto market was to set up an assembly plant in Mexico, with its low wages and good trade access to the United States. After assessing several alternatives, the company identified an existing plant in Guadalajara as the most suitable facility for the new assembly operation. Current owner Grupo Jalisco had put the plant up for sale. Negotiations appeared to be little more than a formality, since commercial real estate values seemed well established through other plants that had recently been sold in the Guadalajara area.

A middle manager representing ALV's worldwide facility management group set up a meeting with the current plant owner, prepared to spend no more than a day or two in the country. In spite of polite introductions and small talk, the initial meeting did not go well. Focused on reaching agreement quickly, ALV had previously submitted a detailed proposal in writing. However, Grupo Jalisco's negotiators had apparently not even read this proposal, since the sales price they demanded as the bargaining began was higher than the Germans' offer by a very substantial amount. The German negotiator sharply rejected the demand, stating that the Mexicans 'could not possibly be serious in asking for such an outrageous sum.' He reminded them of the offer ALV had already made, which he considered very reasonable.

What followed was a fierce competitive bargaining exchange. While Grupo Jalisco's negotiators successively lowered their demands, ALV's offer did not move by much. The company's representative repeatedly emphasized that his opening offer was fair and that he would not raise it unless the other side first provided a reasonable counteroffer. When Grupo Jalisco finally lowered its request by a sizeable amount, he started making small concessions in response, upon which the Mexican team responded with similarly small ones. Though the delta between bidding and asking price was no longer very substantial, subsequent concessions offered by either side were clearly becoming too small to support a mutually acceptable compromise.

More and more agitated over what he called the Mexicans' 'unreasonable behavior,' the German made what he announced as his final offer, suggesting that the Grupo Jalisco team 'take it or leave it.' Again, this did not seem to produce the desired response. The Mexican negotiators instead countered with another small concession. Determined to stay his course, the German threatened to end the meeting and return to his hotel unless Grupo Jalisco accepted his latest offer. Since this did not trigger a clear response either, he ultimately packed up his papers, rose, and left.

The following day, ALV's representative called Grupo Jalisco in order to re-open the negotiation. He was prepared to offer small additional concessions, which he was convinced was all it would take to seal the deal. To his surprise, his counterparts stated that they were no longer interested in negotiating with ALV. The plant later sold to another party for the exact same price the Germans had last offered. ALV's plans to assemble vehicles in Mexico were delayed by several months.

A number of cultural misunderstandings characterize this case. The most significant one may be the failure of both parties to respect each other's pride. The Mexican team might already have been offended when realizing that the German company sent a middle manager, rather than a top executive, to the negotiation. One of the Mexican representatives was probably a senior executive whose expectation was to interact with someone of similar rank. Calling the Mexicans' opening offer extreme and refusing to make meaningful concessions made matters worse. All of this, combined with the lack of opportunity for relationship building with their visitor, led the Mexican team to become increasingly uncooperative and combative. On the other hand, the Mexicans' disregard for the upfront written offer made the German doubt their professionalism. He took the other party's extreme opening offer as a provocation and may have felt that its failure to acknowledge his final offer as serious added insult to injury. Once both sides had dug in their heels, the negotiation exchange was bound to fail.

Recognizing Rules

Many negotiations that fail due to cultural conflict are characterized by a pattern of both sides starting with good intentions, increasingly becoming aggravated, and ultimately finding themselves in a downward spiral that can be very difficult to escape from. Ask international business negotiators about their worst foreign experiences and they may start telling horror stories, the implied message of which is usually that foreign counterparts 'broke the rules.'

Such rules usually represent unspoken expectations that others are required to meet. They may define right and wrong conduct, fair and unfair behavior, acceptable and unacceptable practices. For example, most American negotiators may have expectations of their counterparts such as these: 'never lie,' 'do not get emotional,' 'do not take anything personally,' 'be reasonable' (i.e., 'accept and respond to logical arguments and reasoning'), or 'honor the deals you make' (i.e., 'do not attempt to change or ignore agreements you closed'). While bending such rules might be tolerated to a certain degree, people may cry foul if one is broken. Few emotions change good intentions and positive attitudes faster than feelings of being cheated may. If that happens, the perpetrator is subsequently viewed with mistrust and suspicion. Repeated rule violations frequently tend to leave negotiations in a complete gridlock and often make it impossible for the parties to reach agreement.

The challenge in international negotiations is that there is more than one rulebook. The negotiating parties' views of what is acceptable and what is not may actually differ substantially. For instance, one party might view partial lying, cheating, or getting highly emotional as perfectly normal behaviors when negotiating, while the other may not. Herein lies the dilemma: in any such situation, the rules which negotiators on both sides expect to apply might differ considerably, while the negotiation exchange nevertheless requires the parties to establish and preserve reasonable levels of trust between them. The key to mastering this challenge lies in testing for and recognizing misaligned assumptions, understanding different rule sets, and finding or creating common ground that allows both sides to pursue their negotiation objectives while winning and maintaining each other's trust. Instead of assuming bad intentions or attitudes, negotiators may be able either to modify their behaviors or to openly discuss and resolve conflicting perceptions and expectations with their counterparts.

It's Not Always Culture

As motivational theorist Abraham Maslow once noted, "If the only tool you have is a hammer, you will see every problem as a nail." Even though cultural differences can be found at the heart of many conflicts in international negotiations, a similar caveat applies here.

Negotiation conflicts can be caused by opposing objectives, individual incompatibilities, cultural differences, and other factors. Assuming that learning enough about cultural differences is all it will take to make international negotiations productive and successful would be naïve. Worse, such a mindset could become a mental blindfold that might trigger poor decision-making. Competent negotiators remain aware of cultural stereotypes and use them only as a set of assumptions they question and modify continually when dealing with individual representatives of a given culture. Such individuals may hold values and beliefs that could deviate considerably from the norms of their cultural group. That does not render general observations about cultures useless. However, it explains how conflicts can be caused by individual styles rather than cultural differences. Adding further complexity, real-life experience suggests that cultural and personal values often both influence how individuals negotiate and which rules they expect themselves and others to follow.

All of this only amplifies the need to learn about a culture before engaging in negotiations with any of its members. Understanding cultural differences and preparing for another country's values and preferred styles is not a guarantee for success in international negotiations. Nevertheless, it greatly improves the odds of reaching agreement and builds a foundation for successful collaboration.

Part II: Negotiation Techniques Used Around the World

Unlike the basic concepts presented in Chapter 6, negotiation techniques are specific approaches that are applicable only within a certain negotiation style or in a specific situational context. Negotiators commonly use them to achieve progress towards their strategic objectives and to obtain tactical advantages. We include only those that are commonly used in many cultures, reviewing cultural implications and discussing caveats. We classify them into six different categories:

Chapter 9:   Deceptive Techniques

Chapter 10:   Pressure Techniques

Chapter 11:   Aggressive and Adversarial Techniques

Chapter 12:   Other Emotional Techniques

Chapter 13:   Defensive Techniques

Chapter 14:   Other Negotiation Techniques

This is not a comprehensive catalog, as many other options and variants exist.

Let us start with a few general notes and observations:

• Individual negotiation styles may influence a negotiator's choice of bargaining techniques as much as cultural preferences do. It would be a mistake to assume that all negotiators in a given country will or will not use certain techniques.

• Categories may overlap. For instance, some pressure techniques include deceitful elements, such as when a negotiator makes up artificial deadlines to create time pressure on a counterpart.

- Negotiation techniques are often combined for additional impact, which can make it hard to recognize them. For example, some negotiators employ fake nonverbal messages in order to make their act of showing disinterest in a deal more credible.

- Some of the techniques can be used to counter others. For instance, aggressive behavior often stops if a counterpart threatens in a calm and controlled fashion to walk out otherwise.

Chapter 9: Deceptive Techniques

The primary objective of using deceptive techniques is to conceal one's negotiation strategy and objectives, or to mislead the other side about the value one assigns to the items being negotiated. By withholding such information or by credibly communicating false information, negotiators intend to achieve agreements that favor their position.

Deceptive techniques are used in most cultures around the world. However, in societies where preserving *face* and maintaining strong relationships are important, deceiving a counterpart may jeopardize or destroy long-term business relationships if the party realizes that it is being deceived. In these countries, it is therefore strongly advisable either to refrain from using deceptive techniques or at least to employ only those your counterparts cannot identify as such.

Telling Lies

Negotiators may use outright or partial lies in order to mislead the other party about their strategy or to obtain bargaining advantages. For instance, they may claim that another party made them a better offer for the items being negotiated. This claim aims to make the other side believe that it might lose the deal to another bidder, putting pressure on it to improve its own offer. Another example is that a negotiator might invent reasons why a requested concessions cannot be granted. Lies only work if the other party finds them plausible and assumes that they actually represent the truth.

The first line of defense against lies is to prepare well upfront, collecting and thoroughly verifying relevant information about your counterpart's strategy, intentions, non-settlement options, constraints, and preferred negotiation styles. This will give you a strong foundation for decision making in situations where you think the other might be lying.

Should you suddenly be facing unexpected bargaining obstacles during a negotiation, it is usually best to test whether you are being lied to. In many cases, you can do this by attempting to break through the presumed lie. For example, follow up with several tough questions that challenge the allegation and watch for signs that your counterpart is indeed lying. There could be both verbal and nonverbal clues. Attempting to make their lies more credible, counterparts may use opening phrases such as 'To tell you the truth' or 'Let me be frank' which frequently indicate just the opposite of the intended message. Nonverbal clues include suddenly sitting straight, seeking eye contact where there was little of it before, frequently blinking the eyes, or speaking in a higher pitched voice than before. If you notice any of these clues, assume that you are being lied to. If verbal message and body language do not seem to match up, the nonverbal signals are generally better indicators. Follow up with probing questions if needed. The more pressure you can put on a liar, the more obvious his or her verbal and nonverbal signs will likely become.

Negotiators may use lies in all cultures and in all phases of negotiations. However, it is crucial to realize that definitions of what constitutes a lie and beliefs of when lying is acceptable during negotiations differ substantially across cultures. For example, most people in Northern Europe may agree with a definition of lying as 'not telling the truth.' In contrast, Americans may only agree with a much narrower definition of 'intentionally telling the untruth.' Many of them see nothing wrong with such tactics as omitting crucial information, putting unfavorable terms into easy-to-overlook fine print, making ambiguous statements that imply incorrect conclusions, or even intentionally misleading their counterparts. They might nevertheless be highly offended if another person referred to such behavior as lying.

In cultures where the concept of *face* is very important, such as China, India, Indonesia, Japan, Mexico, or in most Latin American countries, be very careful when asking probing questions in order to detect lies. Even if this makes it harder for you to decide whether someone is indeed lying, you will need to keep your questioning subtle and avoid exerting too much pressure. Unless you convincingly appear to be gathering further information rather than trying to expose a lie, you will risk causing a huge *loss of face* that could be very detrimental for the relationship. In addition, it can be difficult for Westerners to detect nonverbal clues in most Asian cultures, since their members tend to restrict their body language.

In cultures where people generally prefer aggressive negotiation styles, for instance in Israel, Russia, or Ukraine, it may sometimes be effective to directly confront the other party with your belief that its negotiators are lying. Doing so will usually not adversely affect the relationship unless it is done in an adversarial fashion.

Fake Nonverbal Messages

Experienced negotiators may fake nonverbal signals in order to mislead their counterparts about their intentions. Several facial expressions and gestures may help accomplish this. For instance, tightness around the mouth, running one's fingers through the hair, wringing one's hands, or gripping the armrests of a chair are behaviors that will likely be read as signs that the bargaining exchange is not going smoothly. Similarly, negotiators scratching the head, holding their hands together with the palms pointed outward, or folding their arms may send a message of disbelief or rejection. Others who continuously drum their fingers on the table or demonstratively check their watches signal their belief that they are wasting time. Nodding to indicate agreement and shaking the head to signal disagreement may also send strong messages.

Most of these nonverbal signals are designed to make the other side nervous about the state of the negotiation process, pushing it to make further concessions. To be effective, the signals need to follow shortly after the other party has made an offer or proposal.

Fake nonverbal messages may also be used as a distraction designed to confuse the other party. For example, a negotiator may make significantly more or a lot less frequent eye contact than people would normally do, which tends to make the other nervous. Sending a nonverbal message that indicates agreement, for instance by smiling, exhaling, or leaning back, and then unexpectedly stating a sharp 'no' could throw a counterpart off balance.

Deciding whether someone is faking nonverbal messages can be hard, especially if the person has been practicing the technique. It is often best to ask directly, for example by stating 'You seem displeased with my last offer. Please explain why.' Watch the body language when that person replies. If the nonverbal message was indeed a fake one, you will likely see indicators similar to those described under *Telling Lies* (see previous section). Since they have to concentrate on their verbal response, even experienced negotiators are usually unable to control all of their body language and gestures in such a situation.

Negotiators may use fake nonverbal messages in all cultures and in all phases of negotiations. Westerners with limited experience may find it difficult to detect nonverbal messages when dealing with people from many Asian countries. Members of these cultures tend to restrict their body language and may use subtle nonverbal clues, which Westerners may miss entirely.

When using fake nonverbal messages yourself, keep in mind that in some countries, such as Greece or Turkey, gestures and body language may commonly look different from how people in most cultures use them. The intended message may not always be received.

Appearing Weak or Playing Stupid

Negotiators may pretend to be unfamiliar with negotiating in general, new to the industry, or that they lack previous experience with deals like the one under negotiation. Attempting to make their claim more credible, they may wear cheap clothing or otherwise maintain an unprofessional appearance. Some may try to flatter counterparts with remarks such as 'Everybody tells me you are an experienced and fair negotiator' or 'I can clearly see what makes you so successful in everything you do.' Others again may fake illnesses or pretend that they have a weak heart.

Shrewd negotiators may use such tactics throughout all negotiation phases. They will continue to make 'stupid' mistakes if doing so strengthens their position. For instance, they might openly ask what a fair deal would look like, pretending they have no clue. They may frequently change subjects and use lies to instill confusion. When receiving concessions, 'stupid' negotiators may thank their counterparts and praise them for being fair. Next, they may go on to request further concessions, still pretending that they do not know what they are doing.

The technique's objective is to instill a false sense of security, leading a counterpart to let down his or her guard, and/or to win the other's sympathy. If successful, the other party might involuntarily release more information than intended or could become more lenient and collaborative. In some instances, a counterpart may even end up 'protecting' the allegedly inexperienced, weak negotiator, offering better conditions and making more concessions than he or she otherwise might do. Effective negotiators using this approach may be able to get away with very one-sided deals while still making the other party feel good about his or her generosity and fairness.

Executed right, the technique can be surprisingly effective. However, it is pivotal to keep up the act throughout the negotiation. Otherwise, counterparts tend to get suspicious and may react by keeping their information close to the chest and bargaining in more aggressive or adversarial ways.

Dealing with 'weak' or 'stupid' negotiators is often difficult, since they do not have to participate in the normal negotiation process. Unless you are certain that your counterpart is not just acting, you should never allow sympathy to affect your decision-making. Frequently remind yourself of what you consider a fair deal and ask why you would be willing to let the other get anything better than that. Also, realize that the 'stupid' negotiator in effect forces you do all the work during the negotiation exchange, which is anything but fair.

When suspecting that a counterpart is playing stupid, pay particular attention to the early phases of the negotiation. Clearly formulate your opening position. When the 'stupid' negotiator attempts to digress without responding to your offer, ask that person to state and justify his or her own position with equal clarity. The negotiator may attempt to deflect your request by claiming ignorance and switching topics. Do not let the person get away with that. Repeat your request and force him or her to participate in the negotiation exchange. Statements such as 'You must have some idea of what it is you want to get and what you are willing to give up for it' may help make the exchange more constructive.

Playing stupid is rare in cultures where the concept of *face* is very important, such as China, India, Indonesia, Japan, Mexico, or in most Latin American countries. However, negotiators in those countries who are experienced in working with Westerners may use the approach. In contrast, the Japanese will almost never use it. Negotiators from countries such as the Middle East, Turkey, or Russia, on the other hand, sometimes use it with great success, especially when dealing with Americans, Canadians, the British, or Australians.

Westerners, especially Americans, will hardly be successful with this technique. U.S. businesspeople have such a strong reputation around the world that such acting will not be perceived as credible.

Misrepresenting Value

Negotiators sometimes consciously overstate or understate the value of some or all of the items under negotiation. The objective of this technique is to receive more for what they have to offer and/or to give up less for what they want to obtain. Accordingly, such negotiators may either overstate the value of items they do not care about if they think that the other side is interested in them, or they may understate the value of items the other side has that they are interested in themselves.

The best defense against this technique is to conduct a thorough upfront assessment of the other side's objectives. In addition, watch carefully for verbal slips and non-verbal clues that may indicate their real intentions. This can be difficult, so you may have to trust your instincts if you were unable to obtain enough information prior to the bargaining exchange.

This technique may be used in many cultures and can be effective in the information gathering and bargaining phases of negotiations. However, consider that definitions of *good faith* vary greatly across cultures. In countries where honesty is strongly valued in negotiators, such as in the Nordics or in Switzerland, people may have little tolerance for such tactics. On the other hand, members of intense-bargaining cultures, for instance Russians, Turks, Ukrainians, or some Arabs, might be surprised if anyone took offense 'only' because they misrepresented the value of an item.

False Disinterest in Deal

If another party approaches them with a proposal, negotiators sometimes signal right away that they are not interested. If they agree to meet in order to discuss the proposal, they may state that they will do so only as a courtesy to the other, not to indicate that they are willing to make a deal.

Two possible motivations explain such behavior: for one, there might indeed not be much interest to negotiate, which means that reaching agreement may require considerable salesmanship. The more likely alternative, though, is that the party signaling a lack of interest does so only to achieve a favorable opening position. They could actually be quite interested but may be trying to force their counterparts to make an attractive offer. If successful, continuing to show little interest throughout the negotiation might repeatedly allow them to obtain one-sided concessions.

When dealing with a counterpart who pretends not to be interested, never open with an attractive offer. Instead, ask the person under which conditions he or she would be interested in making a deal. It may help to state that from your experience, whether a deal is of interest or not always depends on its terms and conditions. Wait until an answer is formulated and use it to open a more serious negotiation exchange. Alternatively, start with a low offer. Do not make it insultingly unattractive, but keep it below what you think the other party may find acceptable. When you receive an immediate rejection, ask what your counterpart would consider a realistic and attractive offer. Doing so usually allows the negotiation to become more constructive, even though the other side may continue pretending to be disinterested.

False disinterest can be most useful in the information gathering phase of a negotiation but may occasionally also be effective in the bargaining phase. The approach can be employed in any country. This includes cultures whose members generally enjoy bargaining, though they will usually just use it as a starting maneuver that may be quickly dropped. The technique is popular in France, where negotiators can be particularly good at making their counterparts feel like petitioners and may keep up this attitude throughout the negotiation.

False Disinterest in Concessions

This is a variant of the technique described in the previous section: negotiators who just received a major concession may pretend that they are not interested in it, even though they will secretly add it to their list of agreed items and terms. Unless the other party catches it, this gives them a bargaining advantage without having to reciprocate.

The best countermeasure against this tactic is to take back the concession you just made. A non-offensive way of doing so is to ask how much the concession is worth to the other side, stating that you will take it back and replace it with another offer instead if they do not care about it. The other will be quick to intervene in order to keep the concession if they indeed value it highly.

False disinterest in concessions may be shown in most cultures. The technique is applicable in the bargaining phase of a negotiation. In countries where people generally dislike haggling, such as Australia, Austria, Germany, Switzerland, or the Nordics, the approach is rare because it conflicts with their preference to keep the bargaining exchange as swift and short as possible.

False Demands

Negotiators sometimes request to receive items that they may not be seriously interested in. Such demands serve only as 'sacrifices' during the bargaining process. They are usually included in bundled requests for different concessions and designed in a way that makes them unacceptable to the other side. Accordingly, the other party will most likely shoot down such demands, creating opportunities for the originator to request other concessions 'instead.' For example, a negotiator aiming to get a lower price for a service agreement may request 'free training' from a potential supplier; when refused, he or she may then request to 'receive a 10 percent price reduction in lieu of the training.' Executed right, this approach is often more successful than directly requesting the desired concession.

A caveat is that negotiators must never admit that some of their demands were just tactical, since doing so could considerably weaken their negotiating position. Accordingly, it can be very difficult to backpedal should a counterpart actually agree with a false demand.

The best defense against this technique is to find out upfront what it is that the other side is seriously interested in. If you believe that your counterparts are making false demands, indicate that you are willing to give them what they request and watch their verbal and non-verbal reactions. To avoid locking yourself in, you should make it clear that you are only contemplating the concessions and not yet making them. If the other party suddenly changes topics or indicates that they are willing to accept an alternate arrangement, their demand was very likely a false one.

False demands, which may be brought up in many cultures, can be effective in the bargaining and closure phases of negotiations. Use the technique, and any countermeasures against it, with great caution in cultures where the concept of *face* is very important, for example in China, India, Indonesia, Japan, Mexico, or in most Latin American countries. The risk of causing (or suffering) *loss of face* is considerable. In addition, using the tactic may not help with aggressive/adversarial negotiators from cultures such as Russia or Ukraine.

While they may enjoy rejecting your false demand, having done so will not necessarily make them more conciliatory.

False Concessions

In their initial proposals, skilled negotiators may include demands that serve only as 'bargaining material.' Such demands will be dropped later in the bargaining exchange as apparent concessions to stimulate counterparts to reciprocate with real concessions. This approach is often combined with *Written Offers* (see page 174): the initial written proposal may include clauses that impose 'processing fees,' 'rush delivery premiums,' 'legal fees,' and similar demands. Later, the negotiator may promise 'I will drop the processing fees if you give me [a desired concession] in return.' Such false concessions may mislead inexperienced negotiators into believing that their counterparts are acting fair, even when in reality the deal becomes one-sided.

If you believe that you may be offered a false concession, assess its value to yourself *and* the cost of what the other side is giving up. If your conclusion is that it will not cost the other much to drop the demand, point out that you were not prepared to accept it anyway and emphasize that give-and-take bargaining requires both sides to make true sacrifices.

False concessions are frequent in many countries. The technique can be effective in the bargaining phase of a negotiation, especially in cultures whose members dislike bargaining, such as Australia, Austria, Germany, Switzerland, or the Nordics. However, be careful in cultures where the concept of *face* is very important, such as China, India, Indonesia, Japan, Mexico, or most Latin American countries, as false concessions that are not credible could make you look bad and hurt the relationship.

Good Cop, Bad Cop

Widely known as a police interrogation method, this technique is also commonly used during business negotiations. It requires a team of negotiators to coordinate their roles. The objective of this approach is to soften up the other side and make its negotiators believe that they are getting the best possible deal, even when in reality they may end up with unfavorable conditions.

At least one person, the *bad cop*, needs to act in an aggressive or adversarial fashion. This person or group of people must appear influential and should ideally be positioned as the ultimate decision maker. The remaining team member(s) act in *good cop* roles, appearing to be reasonable and collaborative negotiators who sympathize with the other side's positions.

Throughout the negotiation process, the *bad cop* will put significant pressure on the other party, making unreasonable demands, rejecting concessions and insisting on getting better ones, threatening to cancel the whole deal, sometimes even acting irrationally to intimidate the other party. When the *bad cop* finally remains silent, the *good cop* will try to 'soften things up' while asking for further concessions. The two players may also perform acts when asked to reciprocate, with the *good cop* seemingly having to work hard to get the *bad cop* to agree even with small changes, which will then trigger new demands coming from their side. This cycle could be repeated many times during the bargaining exchange. Executed right, the *good cop* and the other party may end up collaborating to satisfy the *bad cop*, which inevitably favors the team using the technique. When they finally think that they are close to reaching a favorable agreement, the *bad cop* may leave the room for a while, giving the *good cop* an opportunity to propose to 'settle the deal now,' saying that they can agree with terms that represent the best the *bad cop* will ever accept.

The technique can only be effective if the main decision is expected to be made during the same meeting. Should a future negotiation round be required, or if the decision making follows after the meeting, the effectiveness of the tactic is greatly reduced because the other party will likely analyze what happened and may reconsider their position.

If you are dealing with a party that you believe is employing 'good cop, bad cop,' do not confront them with that observation. Doing so will only deteriorate the overall meeting atmosphere, while it is highly unlikely that your counterparts will admit to using the tactic. Instead, focus your energy on not allowing the *bad cop* to control the negotiation. The easiest option is often simply to ignore the person, focus the interaction on the *good cop*. If the *bad cop* was presented to you as the highest-ranking person on the other team, use the countermeasures described under **Aggressive Behavior** (see page 146).

If the other party just rejected a proposal you made, ask the *good cop*, if necessary several times, whether your proposal was reasonable and acceptable. Should the *good cop* agree, you will find yourself in a much stronger negotiating position. Alternatively, if the *good cop* keeps evading and pointing to the *bad cop* as the reason your proposal cannot be accepted, the person will eventually lose credibility and find if hard to continue the act.

This negotiation technique is applicable in the bargaining phase of a negotiation. It could be used in many countries, among them cultures where negotiation styles can be competitive and relationships are only moderately important, such as the United States, Germany, Belgium, and the Netherlands, but also in some strongly relationship-oriented cultures, for instance in Brazil, Greece, the Philippines, or South Korea. Properly executed, the tactic will not necessarily affect the overall relationship between the negotiating companies. However, your side will need to exclude the *bad cop* from future negotiation rounds. In addition, your team needs to prepare well upfront to ensure full alignment, since the tactic can easily backfire if cracks show up between your team members' positions.

'Good cop, bad cop' is rare in most Arab and Asian countries, where people generally prefer to work with fully aligned negotiation teams. Do not use the approach in Japan, since it will only confuse your counterparts. They will most likely stall the negotiation until your team has 're-established harmony.'

Limited Authority

Negotiators may prefer to avoid the overt approach of *Good Cop, Bad Cop*, presented in the previous section, since it tends to put considerable strain on the relationship between the parties. A more subtle and therefore less offensive approach is to claim having limited authority to make decisions. Unlike *Good Cop, Bad Cop*, this variant also allows conducting negotiations individually rather than having to work in a team.

'Limited authority' implies that the person who has sufficient decision-making authority cannot or does not wish to attend the negotiation exchange itself, while the representatives who are at the negotiation table lack the necessary authority to decide major aspects. This creates opportunities to use the absent 'decision maker,' who in reality may not even exist at all, in a role similar to 'bad cop,' making tough demands and generally being uncooperative. In the simplest form of the tactic, negotiators may state 'I'll have to ask my boss for permission' whenever the other party requests a concession they are unwilling to make. Next, they might interrupt the meeting or leave the room temporarily in order to consult with the alleged 'decision maker,' upon which they might return to announce that 'the boss says he cannot agree with what you're asking for.'

Psychologically, this creates a situation in which the negotiation taking place in the meeting room itself may seem cooperative, even though the party using the technique continues to make tough demands and to refuse concessions. In the end, everyone in the room may be collaborating in order to satisfy the tough 'decision maker,' which favors the team using the tactic. Using it can be effective in the bargaining and closure phases of negotiations, and is usually employed late in the process, at a point when the other side is already emotionally committed to the deal. Skilled negotiators may combine it with *Nibbling* (see page 140) to obtain a series of last-minute concessions before they finally agree to close the deal.

When confronted with 'limited authority,' take into account that this does not necessarily represent an explicit negotiation tactic. You might be negotiating with representatives whose authority is indeed restricted, or your counterparts could be using a group process or a series of individual consultations to reach consensus decisions, in which case they will be unable to make major decisions at the negotiation table. The latter is common in many cultures and is very likely the case when negotiating in countries such as China, Japan, Malaysia, the Philippines, Singapore, or South Korea.

If you suspect that your counterparts are indeed using 'limited authority' as a tactic, insist that the person holding the authority to make final decisions join the negotiation. If necessary, threaten that you will otherwise terminate it. In many cases, either the decision maker will get directly involved, or the other representatives will suddenly have the necessary authority to continue the negotiation without needing further approval.

This countermeasure is risky to use in cultures where the concept of *face* is very important, such as China, India, Indonesia, Japan, Mexico, or most Latin American countries. Alternatively, ask the party rejecting your request what alternative it proposes instead. If you continuously demonstrate flexibility to change terms while keeping the value of the negotiated options the same, your counterparts may eventually stop using the technique since it will not be effective.

Lastly, keep in mind that you could sometimes find yourself in negotiation settings in which the final decision-maker refuses to attend while your counterparts at the negotiation table lack sufficient decision-making authority. In such cases, which may be frequent in countries like the Philippines, Russia, or Ukraine, your best option will be to negotiate in an equitable fashion while trying to win the support of your counterparts, whose inputs could and often will strongly influence the other party's final decision.

Crazy Like a Fox

With this technique, negotiators may try to convince their counterparts that they are wholly irrational and unwilling (or unable) to follow logical arguments. This may include behaving in erratic ways, sending fake nonverbal messages, frequently switching between cooperative and hostile attitudes, using illogical arguments, or employing other behaviors that could be interpreted as insane. The tactic's objective is usually to confuse the other party and to stimulate them to agree with one-sided demands.

If a counterpart uses this approach with you, it will be best simply to ignore it, acting rationally yourself throughout the exchange. Remind yourself of your non-settlement options and prepare to walk away if necessary. Once the other party realizes that you are not willing to play their game, it may reconsider its strategy.

This negotiation technique, which can be employed throughout the negotiation process, is rare in all countries around the world. The reason we include it here is to emphasize that in a cross-cultural setting, what may seem irrational to you may not necessarily be viewed the same way by your foreign counterpart. Do not automatically assume that someone is irrational because you would act differently. Many cultural gaps can cause such misunderstandings, for instance if one side's primary focus is on financial gains while the other side's objective is to raise its status.

False Least Favorable Option

This technique is generally rare, since it is only effective with extremely adversarial opponents. Their attitude towards negotiating may be *win/lose*, and they may enjoy rejecting the other side's requests. Negotiators who have to deal with such counterparts could present two alternatives to them, asking for the less-favored option. The adversarial counterparts will probably reject this request, insisting on the remaining option. Since this is what it wanted in the first place, the party using the tactic has thus met its objectives. However, it should be careful not to show any triumph, since doing so would only further deteriorate the negotiation atmosphere.

Another version of the tactic consists of proposing a false worst case. Between several existing options, negotiators may state that any of them is good as long as it is not one they specifically point out, which in reality will be the one they desire. Extremely adversarial opponents may enjoy forcing them to choose that very option, again allowing them to achieve their objective.

This technique can be used in the bargaining and closure phases of negotiations. It may work well in countries where negotiations often become confrontational and very aggressive, such as in Russia or Ukraine. Elsewhere, it may be of some use when dealing with extreme negotiators. Never use it with cooperative negotiators who may agree with the proposed option. You will likely need to backpedal, which could considerably weaken your negotiating position.

Chapter 10: Pressure Techniques

The primary objective of using pressure techniques is to create a situation where the other side's negotiators accept an offer that is on the table, believing that neither their non-settlement options nor the expected outcome should they bargain any further are more favorable. It is sufficient to create a psychological perception for the technique to be effective; the members of the other side only have to *believe* that they have no better choice than to accept the offer.

It is unnecessary to employ an aggressive or adversarial negotiation style to apply pressure techniques effectively. Executed skillfully, they can be applied while continuing to negotiate in a cooperative style.

Opening with Best Offer

After making an initial offer, negotiators may attempt to skip the bargaining phase. They may state that they are disinterested in bargaining and that they are therefore putting their best offer on the table right away. To make the statement more convincing, they may add that they firmly believe that the offer reflects the true value of the item(s) under negotiation and that they are unwilling to pay more or receive less than the stated value.

This technique is most effective early in the bargaining phase of a negotiation since it aims to convince the other side that they will receive no concessions whatsoever. For it to work, the counterpart has to be convinced that it reflects a serious intention and not just a tactic. The less bargaining power counterparts have, the more likely they are to accept such an offer. This also assumes that they are sufficiently interested, believing that the offer is favorable over their non-settlement options. Prior to employing the tactic, negotiators using it therefore need to exploit the information gathering phase of the negotiation to ensure that they understand the value the other side attributes to the item(s) being negotiated. In international negotiations, this can be a risky approach since it is often hard to assess this value correctly.

People from many cultures use 'opening with best offer.' Note that the technique does not necessarily represent a conscious attempt to create pressure. In some cases, it may simply reflect a negotiator's honest preference. In particular, this may be the case with people who generally dislike bargaining, such as Australians, Austrians, Germans, Swiss, or people from Nordic countries. Generally, the less enthusiastic the members of a given culture are about bargaining, the more likely they are to accept. Some may actually like the approach since they appreciate the opportunity to cut the bargaining phase short.

Members of cultures where aggressive negotiating is generally preferred, for example Russians or Ukrainians, may also like this technique. They may use it only as a tactic to try out, quickly recovering if they find that it does not work with a given counterpart.

Because of these cultural variances, no single countermeasure exists that would work in all countries. If you believe that the other side uses the approach as a tactic and that it is willing to bargain if you refuse, it is best to simply ignore the offer, responding with an opening offer of your own instead. However, if you think that your counterparts might be serious about the approach, explain to them why you disagree with their value assessment and how this makes it impossible for you to accept their offer. Once you have done so, find a *face*-saving way to help them focus on further bargaining exchanges.

Do not assume that people have bad intentions when using the approach. Your counterparts may be inexperienced or uncomfortable with negotiating, or this technique may be viewed as perfectly ethical within their culture. Never take it personal if others use this approach.

Using this tactic may be perceived very negatively in cultures where people enjoy bargaining, for example in many Arab countries, Greece, Mexico, Nigeria, or Turkey. People in these countries may interpret the approach as an outright refusal to negotiate, which can be taken as a personal offense. Following emotional instinct rather than rational conclusion, they may decide to walk away even if your offer otherwise appears acceptable to them.

In a variant of 'opening with best offer,' a negotiator may try to apply it only to one of the items in a multi-item negotiation. The bargaining phase would still follow, only with a limited scope. For example, the negotiator could declare that the price of an item is inflexible but that related services, for example warranty terms or training offerings, are negotiable. This approach may have a higher chance of being accepted by the other side and will also be viewed as more cooperative.

Intransigence

This is a tactical variant of the **Best Offer** technique: if the other side refuses an initial offer, the negotiator who made it emphasizes that 'This is the maximum we pay' for the kind of product or services being offered, implying that he or she has made the best possible offer and is unable to make any further concessions.

This technique is most effective in the information gathering and bargaining phases of negotiations. Unlike **Best Offer**, intransigence may also work late in a negotiation when trying to draw a line, especially when negotiating from a position of strength. Large corporations, for example, often employ it when negotiating with individuals or smaller companies.

The tactic creates pressure on the other side to accept whatever is on the table. However, it only works if the other side believes that it has no better alternative.

The most effective countermeasure is to emphasize that the offer made is not acceptable to you, threatening that you will walk away if you receive no further concessions. Once you announced this, remain silent and wait for a reaction. However, only use this response if you are indeed prepared to terminate the negotiation. Otherwise, your best option may be to accept what is being offered.

You will rarely encounter, and should not attempt to use, intransigence in cultures where people enjoy bargaining, such as Egypt, Greece, Iran, Mexico, Nigeria, or Turkey. People in these countries often view this approach as a refusal to negotiate, which many of them consider highly inappropriate. An intransigent approach may be received more favorably in countries where people generally dislike bargaining, such as Australia, Austria, Germany, the Nordics, or Switzerland. Members of these cultures may often use the tactic themselves.

Silence

As a way to reject a request for concessions or an offer, negotiators may sometimes remain completely silent. They will look serious, without grimacing, flinching, or otherwise sending non-verbal messages. In order for the technique to be effective, negotiators need to remain silent until their counterparts finally say something, even if this takes several minutes.

The objective of this tactic is to signal displeasure and create pressure on the other side to improve its offering. A negotiator using the technique attempts to advance his or her position, hoping that the other side either makes concessions in order to receive a more positive response or volunteers further information, giving in to an urge to 'justify' an apparently offensive position.

Never make additional concessions only because your negotiation counterpart remains silent. If you believe that others are using this technique with you, first, remain silent yourself. Keep in mind that you might be misreading their intentions; they could be contemplating your last offer or they might be distracted by something else. After an extensive period of silence, when you are certain that your counterparts use it as a tactic, calmly ask whether they plan to respond to your proposal. Avoid doing this too soon; let at least a minute or two pass before speaking again. If the silence continues, explain after a while that you are about to leave because they are apparently not interested in your proposal. Get up and walk towards the door. Assuming that your counterparts continue to be interested, they will stop you before you have left the room. At that point, the pressure is on them to explain their position and make a counterproposal.

Silence can be an effective technique in the bargaining and closure phases of negotiations. Shrewd negotiators in many cultures often use it. Since remaining silent rarely jeopardizes relationships, some may simply try the tactic to see whether it works with their negotiation counterparts. Worst case, it may temporarily affect the atmosphere of the negotiation, but it is usually easy to recover if necessary.

The tactic works well in communication-intense cultures where being silent is interpreted as sending a negative message. It can be an exceptionally powerful negotiation tool in the United States and Ireland, may be effective in countries like Argentina, Mexico, France, Italy, or Spain, and might work in Canada, Hong Kong, Singapore, Taiwan, and many other countries. However, members of some of these cultures can be very patient, so expect that it may take two minutes or more before your counterparts say something, realizing that the negotiation will otherwise come to a standstill. The technique does not have an impact in countries where silence is appreciated, for example in Finland. Keep in mind that silence is a normal part of conversations in many cultures, which may limit its usefulness as a tactic.

Final Offer

Attempting to convince their counterparts that they will receive no further concessions, negotiators may state something like 'This is my final offer' or 'This is the best I have to offer; take it or leave it.' The goal of this maneuver is to induce fear of losing the deal, thus creating pressure for the other to accept. Two important conditions must exist for this technique to work. For one, the other side has to be sufficiently interested in the offer. If its negotiators do not view it as preferable over their non-settlement options, they will decline, which either means that the deal is off or that the party making the 'final' offer has to make further concessions, leaving its representatives in a weakened negotiating position. In addition, final offers have to be credible, convincing the other side that its members will not get any better future offer. Otherwise, they may decide to 'call the bluff.'

It is best only to make final offers late in the game, especially when dealing with inexperienced negotiators. If the others are already mentally committed, their self-induced psychological pressure to 'not lose the deal' may lead them to believe that an offer is if it reflects no more than an attempt to bluff them.

Your best countermeasure when receiving a final offer is simply to ignore it. Re-state your own previous position, or make a different offer instead. If your counterparts are indeed serious, they will repeat several times that their offer is final. Otherwise, they will continue to bargain, realizing that they cannot pressure you into accepting their offer.

Final offers are frequent in many countries. The technique can be effective late in the bargaining phase, but also in the closure phase of a negotiation. In cultures where people enjoy extended bargaining, for instance in many Arab and Latin American countries, Indonesia, or Nigeria, one should not make a final offer until several rounds of bargaining have been completed. Otherwise, people may interpret the tactic as a refusal to negotiate in good faith. Strongly competitive or adversarial negotiators, for instance Israelis, Russians, or Ukrainians, are generally distrustful and reluctant to accept if your final offer comes too soon. Even if they consider it acceptable and think it may be the best one they will get, they might still not accept. In these cultures, many people believe that only extended, tough negotiations lead to good deals.

Generally, the less enthusiastic people within a given culture are about bargaining, the sooner they may accept final offers. Negotiators in countries such as Australia, Austria, Germany, the Nordics, or Switzerland may view final offers as opportunities to speed up the negotiation. Especially if they have only limited international experience, they may not believe that the other side could be bluffing, since they would only state final offers themselves if they were serious.

Final offers may often be bluffs in cultures where people either prefer an aggressive negotiation style, like Bulgaria, Israel, Russia, or Ukraine, or where they prefer tough bargaining, for instance in China, Korea, or in many countries in the Middle East. Never get upset because of this. Your counterparts may consider it a 'bargaining trick' and expect you not to take any of it personally.

If you are willing to 'play hardball,' another possible countermeasure when confronted with a final offer is to respond with a final offer of your own. It can be advantageous to combine this with a threat to walk out, linked to a time limit. For example, if a negotiator stated that his or her final offer is one million dollars, your response might be 'Your offer is completely unacceptable to me. I will not pay a cent more than $950,000. You have ten minutes to accept; otherwise, our negotiation is over.' Even experienced negotiators may sometimes be taken by surprise by such a response. It may convince them that it is best for them to offer further concessions rather than letting you walk out. Never use this approach if you are bluffing – it will ruin your negotiating position if you end up having to backpedal from such a confrontation. Since this maneuver is perceived as adversarial, you should also not use it when negotiating with members of strongly relationship-oriented cultures, such as China, Egypt, Greece, Indonesia, Malaysia, or Singapore.

Time Pressure

In task-oriented societies where people strongly value near-term achievements, such as the United States or Canada, time and deadlines can become important factors in negotiations. Since there is a high sense of urgency and a desire to 'close the deal' fast, many negotiators from these countries become more willing to make concessions when their deadline is approaching. Deadlines can either be self-imposed, for example if the person had planned to spend only a certain amount of time negotiating, or they may be dictated by external constraints. Examples for the latter are alternative offers that expire by a certain date, target dates imposed by management ('I need you to close this deal before the end of the quarter'), or conflicting arrangements, for instance if spending more time in the current negotiation means that the negotiator misses a subsequent meeting with another contact or a flight back home.

Shrewd negotiators in several cultures may exploit every opportunity to apply time pressure when negotiating with Americans or people from other fast-paced societies. Knowing about deadlines the other side is working against can give them a valuable advantage. One popular tactic in countries like Japan, South Korea, or China is for office staff to inquire about a foreign negotiator's or negotiation team's flight arrangements. The reason given may be to 'reconfirm travel arrangements in order to ensure that everything goes smoothly.' This is rarely the true motivation. Rather, the local negotiators now have an advantage, since they know when the other side will start feeling time pressure. They will not hesitate to leverage this knowledge, sometimes in drastic ways.

As an example, assume that you are arriving in China for a negotiation with a local company. You allowed two full days for the exchange, which should give both sides ample time to reach agreement. You plan to return home after the two days. Upon learning about your schedule, your Chinese negotiation partners may fill the first day with lengthy introductions of the company's history and explanations of its organization, operations, products, markets, and other presentations. They may take you out for a long lunch, give you an extensive factory tour, and arrange an evening banquet with numerous toasts and friendly conversations but no opportunity to discuss business. On the second day, they may suggest that you explain your proposal in depth, asking numerous questions and spending considerable time discussing minor aspects of terms and conditions that bear little or no relevance to the outcome of the negotiation. It may not be until late in the afternoon of the second day that they commence with the core negotiation. By that time, with only a few hours left before your scheduled departure, you will be under considerable time pressure and thus more likely to agree with less-than-favorable terms. While some cultures may view such an approach as unethical, the Chinese and others see nothing wrong with it. They use it often with great success.

Another approach that creates time pressure is to request changes to a pending agreement very late in the game. Russian, Ukrainian, Taiwanese, and negotiators from several other cultures often use this. Again, this variant requires that the negotiators using it know the other side's deadline. The requested changes will be more substantial than what they really hope to achieve, creating new bargaining room for them. The party that is under time pressure may be more amenable to making at least some concessions at this late point, since its only other options are now either to miss the deadline or to end the negotiation unsuccessfully.

Time pressure may not always be applied in order to exploit a counterpart's sense of urgency. Some negotiators use it primarily to determine how committed to a prospective deal the other party is. Either this could give them strategic advantages over the further course of the negotiation, or they might be testing the strength of the business relationship.

Your best defense against such time pressure techniques is patience and proper preparation. By setting aside ample time for the negotiation process, not allowing yourself to be pressured by deadlines, and being willing to return for a continuation of the negotiation if schedule conflicts get in the way, you can shield yourself from any time pressures the other side may attempt to apply. Your second best defense may be to avoid giving the other side opportunities to use deadlines against you. Either you may achieve this by not revealing details of your schedule or you may let your counterparts know, often more convincingly, that you have put aside plenty of time should the negotiation take longer than expected and that your travel arrangements can easily be changed. Using this approach, you will likely find the other side conducting the negotiation more swiftly.

This technique is most effective in the closure phase of negotiations. However, it works best when negotiating with people from fast-paced cultures where 'time is money,' such as the United States or Canada. In strongly relationship-oriented cultures where people allocate considerable time for negotiations, such as China, Egypt, Greece, Indonesia,

Malaysia, or Singapore, one risks offending the other side's negotiators, since they may interpret the tactic as a lack of interest or as unwillingness to 'play by the rules.'

Expiring or Decreasing Offers

In addition to the time pressure techniques described in the previous section, there are a number of more overt approaches to put pressure on a negotiation party in order to obtain concessions or drive a deal to closure. One of them is to make an expiring offer that is valid only for a limited time, implying that otherwise the opportunity will be gone. Since this arrangement forces the buyer to make the seller's deadline the buyer's deadline also, the technique can be effective by stimulating quick decisions. As an example, many American companies add clauses to their formal offers that hold them to the offer for a given time period only. It is usually expected that the offering party continue to be interested in the arrangement beyond the expiration date of the offer. However, informing the other side that you will indeed not renew your offer can create time pressure if you convince them that you are serious.

If done in an outright adversarial fashion, this technique is usually referred to as an *ultimatum*. Smart negotiators create counter-pressure by insisting that they will leave the negotiation unless the deadline is extended.

Decreasing offers employ hardball tactics that some negotiators may consider outright hostile. The basic principle is to offer the other party certain conditions only for a defined time period, after which the terms start getting worse. In its simplest version, this could be 'I offer you $10,000 for this item today, but I will only offer $9,500 tomorrow.' The fact that the 'clock is ticking' increases the pressure on the other side to accept the terms offered. There is no effective countermeasure to this tactic if the offering side indeed is willing to walk away from the deal. You can only hope that the technique represents a bluff. Since it is openly adversarial, you may encounter this technique in countries where aggressive negotiation styles prevail, such as Russia or Ukraine, but rarely in cultures that prefer a win-win approach to negotiating.

Using decreasing or expiring offers can be effective if you believe a buyer is generally attracted to your offer but still wants to 'shop around' for alternatives. Ideally, your offer will convince the buyer to make a fast decision in your favor. However, you have to be willing to walk away from the deal if that does not happen. Otherwise, the buyer will call your bluff, continuing the negotiation from a considerably stronger position.

Making decreasing or expiring offers can be useful in the closure phase of negotiations. Using them in international negotiations can be dangerous, though. Employ them only when negotiating with people from highly achievement-oriented cultures, such as Canada or the United States, from cultures that tolerate adversarial styles, such as Israelis, Russians, or Ukrainians, or in situations where you have attractive alternatives such that you do not want to pursue a deal with the current party unless it moves fast. When negotiating with members of strongly relationship-oriented cultures, such as China, Egypt, Greece, Indonesia, Malaysia, or Singapore, using such techniques can be disastrous and must be avoided.

Nibbling

When agreement seems close and both sides appear committed to making a deal, negotiators may attempt to gain further concessions by repeatedly demanding additional 'small' changes. They may say something like 'I could agree to close the deal if only you would accept this concession.' At times, they may combine the tactic with the *Limited Authority* technique, for instance by claiming that their boss will not let them close the deal unless they receive a particular commitment. Experienced negotiators may nibble repeatedly and can be surprisingly effective in doing so. Their effectiveness depends on whether the other side is mentally committed to making the deal. Since nibbling is done late in the game, usually in the closure phase of a negotiation, it also often creates time pressure, which may further increase the likelihood of getting additional concessions.

If a counterpart appears to be nibbling, ask yourself whether you really believe that the person will drop the deal if you refuse to agree with the requested changes. The answer is frequently 'no.' If you have reasons to make further concessions, for instance in order to nurture the relationship or to prevent loss of *face*, ask the other side to reciprocate.

Negotiators in cultures where people like bargaining and haggling frequently use this technique to gain advantages in the final phases of a negotiation. Some, for example Chinese or Koreans, may even do so after a contract has already been signed. Since nibbling generally does not affect the relationship, there is little risk associated with using the technique yourself. Avoid excessive nibbling in cultures where people strongly dislike haggling, such as Australia, Austria, Germany, Hungary, the Nordics, or Switzerland. You will rarely experience members of these cultures using this tactic.

Persistence

This technique requires being patient and persistent with a negotiation counterpart, while not making any significant concessions. Especially in the closure phase of a negotiation, when both sides are mentally committed to the deal and only seemingly small disagreements remain, the side that remains the most persistent usually ends up with the better deal. It is usually counterproductive to rush the end phase of a negotiation, and persistence often pays big rewards.

When using this technique, avoid getting obsessed over the risk of pushing the other side into second-guessing the deal. Once your counterparts are mentally committed to it, which assumes that all relevant obstacles have been removed, they may find the 'unnecessary' hold-ups over small issues annoying but will rarely walk away.

Persistence can have effects similar to *Time Pressure* on people from fast-paced cultures where 'time is money,' such as the United States or Canada. Members of most other cultures view it as less offensive, though, and the risk of offending your counterparts is low as long as you remain willing to make small concessions if necessary.

This technique is most effective in the closure phase of negotiations but may also work in other phases. There is no effective countermeasure other than being equally patient and persistent. Once the other side realizes that you are not likely to 'lose it' and give up something of significant value, its members usually become more cooperative.

Members of cultures where people typically have a low achievement orientation, for instance Russia, may not use this approach intentionally but may still make foreign negotiators feel pressured. Russians and others can sometimes wear out foreign negotiators simply through their seemingly unlimited patience and persistence, coupled with an apparent 'don't care' attitude. The only effective countermeasure is to allocate plenty of time for the negotiation, being equally patient and persistent.

Creating Physical Discomfort

Some negotiators seek to create pressure on their counterparts by making them physically uncomfortable. They may use conference rooms that are too warm, too cold, too small, or too noisy, serve no food or beverages during extended meetings, or find other ways to affect the physical well-being of their counterparts. They make sure that the unfavorable conditions come as a surprise, depriving the other party of its chances to prepare accordingly. The objective is similar to the *Time Pressure* technique: to stimulate the other party to end the negotiation as soon as possible by making greater concessions than its members might be willing to make otherwise.

Your best countermeasure if someone uses this approach is to ask in a non-aggressive way that the condition be changed. If your request is refused, either you can try to relax and ignore the issue, or you could state that you are too uncomfortable to continue the negotiation, suggesting to reconvene later at a place where you have some influence over the meeting atmosphere, such as a hotel conference room. It is essential to make this request in an apologetic manner and to avoid appearing aggressive or disrespectful.

Unlike *Time Pressure*, creating physical discomfort can be effective with people from many cultures. People from countries where negotiation styles are often somewhat aggressive, for instance Russians, Ukrainians, Israelis, the Chinese, or Koreans, are most likely to employ the technique. However, members of many other cultures may also use this approach.

Chapter 11: Aggressive and Adversarial Techniques

This chapter discusses negotiation techniques that members of many cultures may consider aggressive or adversarial. Depending on the cultural context, the word *aggressive* can take on multiple meanings. In the United States, it often has positive connotations, such as 'assertive, bold, and energetic.' However, Americans also understand another interpretation that is common in most other cultures and that we will use in this chapter: 'behaving in angry and violent ways.' The primary objective of using aggressive or adversarial techniques is to intimidate the other side, creating psychological pressure on its members to end the situation by agreeing with unfavorable terms.

In many cultures, for instance in Japan, Thailand, India, Mexico, or in most European and Latin America countries, the overt use of aggressive or adversarial negotiation techniques indicates that either the negotiating partners had no working relationship to begin with, or that it has broken down. However, it is important to realize that people in some cultures may see no contradiction in employing aggressive or adversarial techniques while maintaining and continuing to value strong relationships with the same counterparts. Countries where this attitude is frequent include Brazil, China, and South Korea. Somewhat surprisingly, members of cultures where negotiations tend to become confrontational, such as Russia or Ukraine, may also have this attitude. In the heat of a confrontation, it will be vital to remember that your counterparts are unlikely to have adversarial intentions, assuming that your relationship with them is strong.

Aggressive Behavior

Negotiators employing this technique may display a wide array of different behaviors that serve to seize control of the negotiation and dictate the agenda as well as terms of agreement. Negotiators behaving aggressively may attack personal integrity and professional competence of their counterparts, reject offers as unreasonable and insulting, shout and yell to instill fear, and so on. They often hope to intimidate weaker counterparts, with the goal of receiving additional concessions. To be credible, they have to use the tactic right from the start of the negotiation. Aggressive behavior may not always be a conscious tactic since it could also reflect a natural inclination.

When dealing with an aggressive negotiator, it is important to remain patient. Remember the old adage that 'dogs that bark do not bite.' Listen and watch carefully for leaks and non-verbal messages that may provide valuable information about your counterpart's objectives. It is usually best to remain quiet until he or she asks you to say something. When you finally do, calmly say that you are not finished in case you are interrupted. If necessary, point out that you did not talk while the other was speaking and that you now expect the same courtesy.

If your counterpart is behaving in an outright adversarial fashion, first try to calm things down. For example, you might use an excuse to call a short break. If the adversarial behavior continues after the break, which usually indicates the use of a technique rather than a state of emotion, state clearly that you will not participate in any further discussions unless conducted in a professional manner. If necessary, announce that you are taking another break and that you will terminate the negotiation if the person does not resume it in a professional manner afterwards. While it does create a risk of having to walk away, this approach will frequently make the negotiation more productive.

Russians and Ukrainians may employ aggressive behavior in all phases of negotiations. Negotiators in several other Central and Eastern European countries as well as Israel sometimes also resort to this technique. However, never use it in cultures where the concept of *face* is very important, such as China, India, Indonesia, Japan, Mexico, or most Latin American countries, even when your counterparts may seem to be employing it themselves. They will likely resume negotiating in a more cooperative fashion after a while.

A variant of this approach is referred to as 'passive-aggressive behavior.' Here, negotiators may completely refuse to cooperate with their counterparts. They may not actively engage in the process and show aggressive reactions to the other side's bargaining attempts. Unlike the *Fake Disinterest* technique discussed earlier, negotiators employing this approach, who usually have a distaste for bargaining, are not interested in the negotiation process and thus see no reason to participate in it. However, that does not mean that they will not be interested in reaching a deal.

The best way to deal with passive-aggressive behavior is often to propose a follow-up meeting, asking the person to prepare a contract proposal as a basis for discussion. Come to the next meeting equipped with your own written version. At that point, there are three possibilities: first, your counterpart may not have prepared any proposal, which gives you a chance to make your version the basis for discussion. Second, your counterpart may have a proposal that looks reasonable, in which case it is best to accept it. Third, your counterpart may have included clauses that you disagree with, in which case you could try to trade clauses between the two versions on the table where feasible. Either way, the fact that you now base the bargaining on written documents with clearly defined options makes the negotiation easier and likelier to proceed in a productive fashion.

Passive-aggressive negotiating, which affects all phases of the process, is not very culture-specific. People who generally dislike bargaining and do not view business relationships as very important are somewhat likely to take this approach. Generally, passive-aggressive behavior is rarely an effective negotiation technique unless the other side is very inexperienced.

Extreme Openings

Earlier in this book, we mentioned the importance of setting high aspirations, emphasizing that they must nevertheless be rationally defensible. Negotiators who use extreme openings, that is, initial offers that are difficult to defend rationally, do not intend to reveal their aspirations by doing so. They use the tactic to trigger reactions from the other side. For instance, they may start by offering one-fifth of the true value of an item they are interested to buy, hoping that their counterparts will react by stating that they 'expect at least $10,000' or 'ask for no less than 9,000,' for example. Extreme offers often provoke at least subtle reactions that can inadvertently provide valuable information and clues. Another motivation for the technique may be that the party using it does not have a clear idea of what a reasonable offer might be. Again, by making one that is 'unreasonable,' they hope to receive clues about their counterparts' expectations. The technique of using extreme openings may lead to one-sided deals if the other party has no idea of the true value of an item under negotiation. Antique dealers can make fortunes with this approach if clueless buyers accept their extreme initial offers.

If someone confronts you with an extreme opening, react first by showing complete shock, then point out that the offer you received is completely unrealistic. You might add that if the other party is indeed serious, you will be unable to make a deal with them. Insist on getting a *serious* offer instead. It is vital not to back off if this request is refused. If necessary, state that you are unwilling to enter into the negotiation process unless your counterpart makes a reasonable offer. If there is still no progress, make an equally unrealistic counteroffer that is extreme at the other end of the spectrum, then point out that both sides have made unrealistic offers and promise that you will respond in kind if you receive a realistic one. Another effective countermeasure may be to ask *Probing Questions* (see also page 167). This often works because your counterpart will be struggling to come up with a rational explanation to defend its offer.

Always dismiss extreme openings and consider your counterpart's second offer as his or her starting position. Otherwise, you might fall into the mental trap of feeling compelled to make big concessions yourself if the other moved far from their initial unrealistic position. When using extreme openings yourself, never offer a second bid because your counterpart rejected the initial opening as 'not good enough.' Instead, request to get a counteroffer.

The technique is only useful at the beginning of the bargaining phase. Its effectiveness depends hugely on the cultural context. In countries where relationships are critically important, for example in China, Indonesia, Malaysia, or Singapore, and in cultures where people generally dislike haggling, such as Australia, Austria, Germany, Switzerland, Hungary, or the Nordics, making extreme opening offers is often viewed as overly aggressive or adversarial. Members of these cultures may become very upset if someone uses the approach. In extreme cases, they may choose to terminate the negotiation. People in several other countries, for instance in Central Europe, also tend to dislike the approach but usually do not take it as negatively as the above group.

On the opposite end of the spectrum are cultures whose members enjoy haggling, such as most Arab countries, Indonesia, Nigeria, Pakistan, the Philippines, or Turkey. People in these cultures may think the technique perfectly acceptable and usually have no bad intentions when using it. Never interpret the tactic as an adversarial step. Instead, keep cool and try to maintain a positive attitude.

Anger

Negotiators using this technique may openly display angry behavior, for instance by raising voices or showing angry mimics and gestures, attempting to pressure the other side into making concessions. Rather than trying to create intimidation as *Aggressive Behavior* does, the purpose of this technique is to convince the other side of the seriousness of a position and to leverage most humans' inclination to compromise as a way to prevent conflicts from escalating. Competent negotiators use the tactic in a controlled manner, never losing their temper. However, for it to be effective, it is important to convince the other side that its members are indeed facing a serious outburst of temper. Some people may combine it with a *Walkout* (see page 153) for added psychological impact.

When confronted with angry behaviors, it is vital not to respond in kind. Stay calm and friendly, and remind yourself that you may be facing an intentional tactic, not an emotional reaction. Watching your counterpart's body language may help determine whether it is an act or not. In parallel, listen carefully for verbal leaks; even experienced negotiators may inadvertently reveal valuable information during this phase since few humans have the mental capacity to carefully choose their words while 'acting.' If you remain calm enough, it will become embarrassing for your counterpart at some point and he or she will be struggling to find a believable way to calm down. When the behavior finally stops, point to your recent concessions and ask how they could get so aggressive with someone who showed such a willingness to cooperate. You may be able to make them feel guilty and obtain concessions.

This technique is most effective in the bargaining and closure phases of negotiations. Russians and Ukrainians in particular use it often and may be masters at 'playing the act' in a convincing manner. The tactic can also be effective in many other European countries, the Middle East, the United States, or in Canada, even though members of these cultures will rarely use it themselves.

Generally, the effectiveness of this technique depends mostly on how important *face* and personal pride are in a given culture. People in the Nordics, for example, rarely use it and may become very uncomfortable if someone else does, though outbursts of anger will not necessarily damage the overall negotiation. In contrast, it is usually counterproductive to display anger openly in any of the South or East Asian countries, as well as in most of Latin America, where doing so can cause *loss of face* and respect.

Threats and Warnings

Negotiators trying to increase the pressure on their counterparts to accept proposals or make concessions may resort to open threats, informing them that any further refusal to concede certain points will have unfavorable consequences. Threats can be explicit ("We will terminate the negotiation if you do not accept") or implicit ("We will only be able to continue the negotiation if you accept"). They usually aim to convince the other party that the only alternative to accepting a demand is non-settlement.

Threats must be credible for the technique to work. When using the approach, give your counterparts enough information and paint a threatening yet realistic picture of the consequences of them being uncooperative. In addition, threats should reflect serious intentions. Should a threat you made turn out to have been a bluff, your negotiating position will be greatly weakened.

'Warnings' are threats of third-party consequences. Rather than threatening actions under the issuer's immediate control, they imply that others will affect the other side adversely unless they cooperate. For example, negotiators may warn that others will think badly of their counterparts should the proposed deal fall apart. Warnings are usually much less aggressive than threats are and may therefore be more effective.

When faced with a threat, two aspects are important to consider: whether you actually believe it, and whether you regard the consequences of the threat worse than your non-settlement alternatives. If either answer is 'no,' simply ignore the threat. This is almost always better than to challenge it, which bears the risk of hurting the other's pride or causing loss of *face*.

Threats and warnings may be used in many cultures and are most effective in the bargaining and closure phases of negotiations. Applied in a non-aggressive fashion, the technique is acceptable in most European countries, the United States, Canada, and many others. Never take threats or warnings personally. People in countries where negotiations may become confrontational and very aggressive, such as Israel, Russia, or Ukraine, often try to bluff when making threats without worrying about the potential loss of credibility.

How members of *face*-oriented cultures view the use of threats and warnings during negotiations can be confusing. On one hand, many, among them Indians, Indonesians, Japanese, and others, view them as inappropriate and often unacceptable. However, in other Asian countries such as China, South Korea, or Taiwan, as well as many Latin American countries, people may actually use the technique themselves, at least in indirect and more subtle ways. Even if they do, be cautious when using similar tactics yourself in these countries since the risk of damaging relationships can be significant.

Walking Out

Negotiators may use walkouts as an intimidation technique designed to convince the other party that no further concessions will be available to them. They usually do so by announcing that they see no value in negotiating any further, packing their briefcases, and leaving the room. 'Emotional' walkouts are accompanied by demonstrative behavior that may include yelling, making angry gestures, or slamming doors. They should come as a surprise to the other side. An alternative strategy is to use a 'calm' walkout, where the negotiator leaves the room quietly. This variant tells the other side that the behavior does not just reflect a temporary emotional outburst. It is often preceded by threats.

Walking out can be effective with risk-averse counterparts. However, it is always a gamble since the other side may end the negotiation. Smart negotiators never walk out unless they are happy with their non-settlement options.

A less aggressive variant can be used when negotiating as a team. Here, only one of the team members, usually an influential one, walks out at a critical junction of the negotiation exchange. The person remains calm while walking out, but facial expressions and body language convey that he or she is very displeased with the way the negotiation is going. The team members who remain in the room may be able to leverage the psychological pressure this created to obtain concessions from the other party.

If a negotiator walks out on you, never try to keep the person back or run after him or her. It may be effective to let him or her leave and go home yourself. Remain patient and let significant time pass, at least a few weeks. You will likely hear back from the person during that time, asking whether you want to resume the negotiation, in which case you will be in an advantaged position. There is a small risk that you may not hear back from him or her, which means that the negotiation is likely over. Getting in touch yourself inevitably puts you into a much weaker negotiating position, though.

If you do not want to take the risk of the negotiation being over, for instance because your non-settlement options are unfavorable, here is an alternate strategy: when the negotiator starts walking to the door, stop him or her by saying 'I'll give you one more chance.' Never say 'Stop,' 'Wait a minute,' or anything else that may sound like you are desperate for the other to stay. It is crucial to make it sound like you are doing *the other person* a favor by calling him or her back, not the other way around. Next, ask the person to return to the table and get settled again, and decide how you will try to break the impasse. This may include offering a different concession from what the other side has been requesting, which should re-engage both sides in the negotiation without either of them 'giving in.'

Walkouts can be employed in the bargaining and closure phases of negotiations. Russians and Ukrainians use them often, sometimes repeatedly during the same negotiation. People in other countries that are not strongly relationship focused, e.g. in Poland, the Czech Republic, the Netherlands, Germany, or Israel, may also use the tactic. Be cautious when using it with Americans, Canadians, or most Western Europeans, since there is a high probability of your negotiation being over.

Do not use this technique at all in strongly relationship-oriented cultures, which includes most countries in Asia and Latin America. It may be better to employ a 'friendly' walkout instead. If the negotiation seems to have reached a dead end and you are contemplating to end it unless the other side shows willingness to make concessions, start packing up your papers and announce something like this: 'I sense that we will not be able to reach agreement today. Rather than letting this affect our great relationship which I value very highly, I would prefer it if we ended our negotiation

now. Let us please stay in touch and try to find a new opportunity in future that will allow us to work together.' The
basic effect of this approach is similar to a 'calm' walkout: it
forces your counterparts to decide whether to hold you back
or let the negotiation end unsuccessfully. Nevertheless, this
version usually does not damage the relationship and leaves
doors open for a possible future cooperation.

Chapter 12: Other Emotional Techniques

This chapter discusses emotional negotiation techniques that members of most cultures view as neither aggressive nor adversarial. Most of them attempt to trigger emotional reactions as a way to obtain concessions or to motivate the other party to become more cooperative.

Attitudinal Bargaining

Negotiators use this technique to create or reestablish a constructive and cooperative negotiation atmosphere, especially with counterparts whose communication styles and negotiation attitudes are somewhat aggressive. They may smile frequently, subtly emphasize their interest in win-win outcomes of the negotiation, ask about the other side's concerns, and so on. Other actions may include choosing pleasant meeting venues and showing generally courteous behavior.

If none of these actions proves effective and the negotiation exchange becomes tense and aggressive, negotiators may state their belief that such a meeting atmosphere will adversely affect either side's ability to reach their objectives. They may ask directly what they can and what the other side is willing to do to make the exchange more productive, becoming quite forceful if needed. If a combative opponent's behavior still does not change, they may tell the other clearly that they will terminate the negotiation unless he or she returns to more civilized conduct.

Attitudinal bargaining can be effective in all phases of negotiations. Its impact may be small or negligible in cultures that promote adversarial negotiation styles, such as Russia or Ukraine. Nevertheless, the technique can be applied in all cultures with little risk of adversely affecting the meeting atmosphere. Concerns should be expressed very tactfully in cultures where the concept of *face* is important or where personal pride may be a strong factor, such as in China, India, Indonesia, Mexico, or in Latin America.

Dual Messages

Before or after making an offer, negotiators may sometimes send their counterparts dual messages, one that is overt and another that is more subtle and indirect. For instance, a car dealer may show a customer a more expensive car than he or she may be looking for, name the price, and then casually mention that the client probably could not afford this model. An IT service vendor may offer a more comprehensive solution than requested, mentioning to the prospective client that 'This one would give you much more value but probably exceeds your budget.' This approach can result in two effects: it often creates psychological pressure, playing to the other party's pride and challenging the person to opt for a bigger deal than was previously targeted. In addition, it can be an effective way to obtain information, since counterparts often react by revealing their bargaining objectives or limits.

When receiving dual messages, it is usually best to ignore the subtle part altogether. Remind yourself that if the negotiator bringing it up were serious with the comment, it would make no sense to send the message at all. Stick with your negotiating objectives and make it clear that you will not digress from them.

This technique can be useful in the information gathering and bargaining phases of negotiations. People in many countries may sometimes employ it. However, it is rare in cultures where the concept of *face* is very important, such as China, India, Indonesia, Japan, or Singapore, and in countries where relationships are critical, for instance in China,

Indonesia, Malaysia, or Singapore. In these countries, the secondary message should be very subtle. Otherwise, you risk offending your counterparts and severely damaging the relationships.

Guilt and Embarrassment

Negotiators often try to make their counterparts feel guilty or embarrassed, hoping that this will stimulate them to make further concessions. Four variants can be effective:

- If the other party made an unreasonable demand, for instance by opening with an extreme offer, negotiators may explain calmly how unrealistic the proposal is. The effect can be intensified by pointing out how they had been looking forward to the negotiation or how disappointed they are by the unfair demand. They will then fall silent, which often increases the other's discomfort. When dealing with a cooperative counterpart, the negotiator using the technique may be able to exploit feelings of guilt or embarrassment by directly following with a request for a concession that the other may find difficult to decline. In such a situation, the concession becomes an apology for the behavior.

    If someone uses this technique with you, remind yourself that effective negotiations require that neither side take anything personal. It can be beneficial to point this out to your counterpart as well. However, doing so is risky in cultures where the concept of *face* is very important, such as China, India, Indonesia, Japan, or Singapore. People in these countries rarely use the tactic themselves, since such behavior may cause loss of *face* for both parties involved and jeopardizes existing relationships. Unless the ties with your counterparts are very strong, refrain from using the tactic in these cultures.

- Another way to execute this technique is for negotiators to make repeated demands they know the other side will reject. It is important to strike a careful balance, demanding concessions that go beyond what the other might accept but not so unreasonable that the other could justifiably get upset over them. Once a few such subsequent requests were rejected, they may remark something like 'Come on, you'll have to give me *something*,' attempting to make the other feel guilty for having rejected every one of the requests. This variant can be effective when bargaining with people from *face*-oriented cultures, some of whom may even respond to the initial demands with counterproposals of their own.

  When confronted with this tactic, respond to the second round of demands with an observation that the parties must have different beliefs of the true value of the items being negotiated. Then, explain why you think the demand is unreasonable, and emphasize how much you are interested in finding a fair solution for both sides. This response will likely throw your counterpart off balance and may even create some embarrassment on his or her side.

- In an approach that is inverse to the previous one, negotiators may make several small concessions in a row. For example, they may successively drop their price in a series of apparently one-sided concessions from $1,000 to $980, then to $970, and then to $950. Next, they may suggest that they already made several price moves and that they will be unable to move down any further. The objective of this variant is to make the other party feel guilty about accepting several concessions without reciprocating, which could make them more likely to accept an unfavorable agreement.

  If someone makes such repeat concessions when negotiating with you, take them as a single move rather than several steps. What matters is how far overall your counterpart has moved, not how many steps it took to do so. Whether or not you consider the total significant should guide your response, but it will be important to point out that you are taking your counterpart's 'several moves' as only one.

- If a significant gap exists between both sides' latest proposals, negotiators may propose to 'split the difference,' suggesting that both agree instead to meet in the middle between their respective positions. On the surface, this may seem fair. However, more often than not, such a suggestion will come from the party that has more to gain, that is, whose position is farther away from the true value of the item or items being negotiated. Rejecting such a proposal can make the other party feel guilty even when they sense the imbalance.

  Should a counterpart use the approach with you, think carefully about both parties' previous moves and concessions. If you believe that you previously moved further toward a reasonable compromise than your counterpart did, meeting in the middle would give the other an unfair advantage, so reject the suggestion. Emphasize that you are very interested in making the deal fair and explain why you do not believe that splitting the difference would do both sides justice. Ask the other party to make a different suggestion, or make a counterproposal yourself.

Techniques to create guilt and embarrassment are most effective in the bargaining and closure phases of negotiations. In addition, they may occasionally help when trying to reach closure. In general, be careful when using them in cultures where the concept of *face* is very important, such as India, Indonesia, Japan, Mexico, or most Latin American countries. When rejecting a request, it will be important in these countries to send strong signals indicating that you value the relationship highly and that you are searching for a solution that both sides can feel good about. For instance, make counter-offers that include a concession (and ask for one in return).

Grimacing

Negotiators may grimace, flinch visibly, or look dejected as an indication that they are not in agreement with an offer or proposal they received. They usually remain silent afterwards, which serves to underline the message. The objective of this technique is to signal rejection in a not-too-aggressive way and to stimulate the other side to improve its offer. While this technique is similar to *Silence*, it includes an emotional component that can make some counterparts feel guilty.

If someone uses this behavior with you, ignore it and refuse to accept it in lieu of a response. Simply remain silent until the other person ultimately says something. If the silence continues for an extended time, use the same strategy as with the *Silence* pressure tactic: calmly ask whether the negotiator plans to respond to your proposal; if necessary, explain that you will leave because there is no apparent interest in it, get up, and start walking towards the door. If there is any interest in continuing the negotiation, your counterpart will stop you, at which point you will have gained the upper hand.

This technique is most effective in the bargaining phase of a negotiation and may be used in many countries. Members of cultures where the concept of *face* is very important, such as the Chinese, Indians, Indonesians, or the Japanese, expect gestures and body language to be very subtle. A dejected look on your face will still send them a clear message, while grimacing may reflect poorly upon you if done too demonstratively.

Appeals to Personal Relationships

Negotiators may appeal to personal relationships when trying to get the other side to agree with a proposal or to make a concession. This may include open hints such as 'You owe me this one for the sake of our friendship' or 'Show me that you value me by agreeing with this request.' They may sometimes use a future orientation by leveraging **Promises** (see also page 169), for instance in statements such as 'Accepting my request will affirm our relationship and give you great advantages in our future business relations.'

This technique attempts to put the other party in a psychological bind by equating rejection of a request with rejection of the overall relationship. This can create a serious dilemma, since the other's desire to obtain the best deal possible will conflict with the intention to build lasting and rewarding business relationships. Finding a constructive way out of this situation can be challenging.

Your best strategy when facing this dilemma is to take a realistic look at the situation. Rationally assess how strong your present relationship with the other party really is, and consider whether you believe that you owe the other side a concession or whether you trust your counterparts to reward you down the road if you agree with the request. As far as future rewards go, set the hurdle high; it is usually best to discard lofty promises and expectations as irrelevant.

Appeals to personal relationships can be effective in the bargaining and closure phases of negotiations. Curiously, this technique is most often employed by people whose culture does *not* value relationships very highly and by people using it only with others with whom they have *not* built strong relationships yet. Negotiators in the Middle East, in Central Europe, and elsewhere may try this approach frequently.

In contrast, the tactic is rare in most countries where relationships are critically important, for instance in China, Indonesia, Malaysia, or Singapore. People in these countries use such appeals only if strong relationships between the parties exist or are likely to emerge. If that is the case, such an appeal represents a promise that your counterparts will very likely live up to at some future point. In strongly relationship-focused cultures, do not appeal to personal relationships yourself unless you are fully committed to the future obligation such a request represents. In addition, be absolutely certain that you and your counterparts both feel good about the state of your relationship. If they reject your request because they feel differently, you lose *face* and are left in a weak negotiating position.

Chapter 13: Defensive Techniques

This chapter discusses effective countermeasures to some of the negotiation techniques described in previous chapters.

Changing the Subject

Negotiators may frequently digress or change subjects during the negotiation exchange in order to distract or confuse their counterparts. The technique's primary objective is to keep the other side from pursuing a systematic strategy and dictating the negotiation agenda. It can also be an effective way to accept concessions without reciprocating or to avoid releasing information.

When dealing with a negotiator using this style, carefully keep track of all commitments made on either side. If your counterpart changes subjects after you just made a concession, ask 'Does the fact that you just changed the topic mean that you do not value the concession I just made?' Should the response be evasive, clearly state before continuing with the new subject that you choose not to commit to the concession under the circumstances.

Changing the subject can be effective in all phases of negotiations. More often than not, the approach may reflect cultural differences rather than an intentional negotiation technique. People in polychronic cultures, for example in France, most of Latin America, the Middle East, and many other countries and regions, may naturally prefer this style and will have no bad intentions even when frequently changing subjects. Attempting to use the technique yourself will rarely be effective in these cultures.

On the other hand, it is not recommended to use the tactic with people from strongly monochronic cultures, such as the United States, Canada, Germany, Switzerland, or the Nordic countries. Priding themselves with being organized and systematic, they are unlikely to use it themselves and may get upset if you do.

Blocking

Negotiators who want to avoid answering sensitive questions often resort to blocking techniques. They may not like to respond if doing so would reveal their negotiation strategy, make it impossible to gain certain concessions, or otherwise give their counterparts a tactical advantage. Several blocking options can be effective. Negotiators may simply ignore questions as if they did not hear them, continuing the discussion. Done innocently enough, their counterparts may not even notice. With questions addressing several aspects, it is possible to focus on those that are easy to cover while ignoring others. Other options include responding to a different question from the one that was asked or giving general answers to specific questions. Politicians often use such tactics to deflect aggressive questions without appearing to be uncooperative.

Another alternative is to respond with a question, for instance by asking 'What would you suggest?' This might throw the other party off balance and put its negotiators on the defensive.

The best countermeasure against negotiators who block is to be very persistent. Asking the same questions over and over makes it hard to continue the approach. At some point, the other party will have to choose whether to give valid responses or to admit that it is unwilling to answer.

Blocking can be useful during the information gathering phase of a negotiation. It may take practicing before you will be able to use the technique effectively. In general, it is applicable in most countries. However, be prepared for people from strongly monochronic cultures, for instance Americans,

Canadians, Germans, the Swiss, or anyone from the Nordics, to repeat their questions persistently. The technique is very unlikely to work in Japan, where most businesspeople will keep repeating their questions until they received satisfactory answers.

Blocking can be very effective in several other countries, especially in those where the concept of *face* is very important. Examples include China, India, Indonesia, Malaysia, and Singapore. For fear of causing loss of *face*, members of these cultures may refrain from repeating their questions. However, do not make your refusal to answer a question too obvious, since this might damage the relationship.

Probing Questions

Negotiators who are unwilling to accept their counterparts' offers may not want to reject them outright. Instead, they could respond by asking probing questions. The objective of this technique is to force the offering party's negotiators to explain the logic behind their proposal, which will ideally lead them to realizing that their offer was inadequate. Executed effectively, the approach is constructive and non-threatening, avoiding the risk of getting stuck because both sides 'dig in their heels.'

Asking probing questions can be an effective countermeasure against **Extreme Openings**. Negotiators using it start by stating their desire to understand the other's rationale, suggesting to jointly go through a detailed analysis of the value of the deal. Someone who just opened with an extreme offer will inevitably fail to find a rational explanation for it, especially if the deal includes several components that need to be explained individually. For instance, when interested in buying a business, the buyer may ask the potential seller who just requested an outrageous amount for it to assign specific values to each of the individual components of the deal, such as the company's buildings, equipment, inventories, and so on. When added up, the sum of these components will be significantly less than the total amount. While probably still exaggerated, these numbers represent a basis for discussing the true value in a more rational fashion.

This technique can be effective in the information gathering and bargaining phases of negotiations. Its value is not limited to situations where the other side used extreme openings. In fact, asking probing questions often helps the bargaining exchange become more rational. Negotiators in cultures who prefer rational problem-solving approaches, such as the United States and Canada, many European countries, or Japan, often resort to this tactic. Be careful when using it in cultures where the concept of *face* is very important, such as India, Indonesia, Japan, Mexico, or most Latin American countries. It could severely damage the negotiation if your questions make the other side look stupid or dishonest.

Directness

Asking very direct and candid questions can be an effective way to find out more about a negotiation party's intentions. For example, when a counterpart just rejected an offer as 'not good enough,' a skilled negotiator may respond by asking 'Ok, so how much are you willing to pay?' or 'What would you consider a fair agreement then?' The approach tends to work best if it comes as a surprise to the other party, since this may lead the other negotiators to openly sharing their intentions and objectives. Using the tactic can be especially valuable immediately after a counterpart has done some initial posturing or expressed a warning or threat. Even if the other party deflects the questioning, directness often helps focus the exchange on a realistic range.

If your counterpart in a negotiation asks you a very direct question that you do not want to answer, simply respond with a neutral statement that leaves enough further maneuvering room, such as 'I believe my previous proposal was fair but am willing to reconsider if you convince me that the value of the deal is higher than I think right now.'

Directness can be useful in the information gathering and bargaining phases of negotiations. It can be particularly effective in countries where people generally dislike bargaining but have a high sense of fairness, for instance in the Nordics. It is also applicable in many other cultures, though. Use it cautiously where the concept of *face* is very important, such as China, India, Indonesia, Japan, Mexico, or most Latin American countries, since directly rejecting the other party's objectives could lead to embarrassing situations. Avoid the tactic in cultures whose members enjoy and expect extended bargaining and haggling, such as in the Middle East, Indonesia, Mexico, or Nigeria, since asking direct questions may insult people who could view this as an outright refusal to bargain.

Promises

One of the most valuable negotiation techniques, making promises can be effective in both offensive and defensive situations. The basic approach is inverse to the **Threats and Warnings** technique described on page 151. Rather than implying a future negative reaction *unless* the other side agrees with a request or proposal, negotiators use the tactic by announcing a positive consequence *if* the other side agrees with their demands. In other words, promises reward affirmative behavior rather than punishing an adversarial one, which often contributes to creating a positive win-win atmosphere for the bargaining exchange. The underlying objective is to convince the other party that agreeing with the request is favorable over any non-settlement outcome.

Promises are normally specific, such as 'If you reduce your asking price by $1,000, I will improve my delivery terms by two weeks.' They must be credible and only work if the other party is confident that the promise will be kept. Unspecific promises, such as 'Trust me, you won't regret it if you agree with this,' are best ignored as they do not meet these criteria. It is vital for negotiators using the tactic to keep their promises. Otherwise, the other side may cry foul and could choose to terminate the negotiation.

Making promises can be effective in the bargaining and closure phases of negotiations. The technique can be used in all countries and is especially useful where the concept of *face* is very important, for example in China, India, Indonesia, Japan, Malaysia, and Singapore. However, it may be less effective in cultures where people are not motivated by future benefits, which includes Nigeria and several other African countries, some in the Middle East, and a few Asian countries such as Pakistan or Thailand. The technique may prove ineffective in cultures whose members view compromise as a sign of weakness, for instance Russia and Ukraine.

Dealing with Inflexible Positions

This technique can be useful when a negotiation has reached a standstill because members of one of the negotiating parties have 'dug in their heels,' refusing to compromise or change their position. Challenging them in such a situation is often of little help and may just add aggravation. Smart negotiators facing such counterparts may instead suggest to review the underlying objectives of the party causing the standstill. They will strive to find out what makes that particular position so important. Analyzing the other's needs and intentions is a constructive approach that can lead to the identification of alternative solutions while avoiding *loss of face* for either side.

For additional impact, it can be beneficial to emphasize areas of agreement between the parties rather than focusing only on areas of conflict. This step may foster the overall relationship and make the areas of conflict seem less critical. However, it is usually not sufficient by itself to eliminate the conflict.

The combined approach can be used in all cultures, including those who favor somewhat aggressive negotiation styles, such as Israel, Russia, or Ukraine. It is applicable in the bargaining and closure phases of negotiations.

Chapter 14: Other Negotiation Techniques

Range Offers

Negotiators who intend to signal their collaborative spirit and willingness to compromise may sometimes base an offer on a value range rather than on a specific number. For instance, they may state something like 'I think this would be worth between 9,000 and 10,000 to me, depending on your terms and conditions.' One scenario in which this approach might work well is if a negotiator does not know the true value of an item but is forced to make an early offer. Since they leave some bargaining room and are often perceived as conciliatory, range offers can be effective with competitive counterparts. An additional benefit is that the extremes of the range imply that this is the lowest or highest the offering party will go, promoting the idea that agreement can only be reached within this range.

Using this technique is not without risks, and experienced negotiators usually prefer to determine the exact amount they want to offer. Range offers tend to make the offering party look insecure, which could stimulate the other party to bargain more competitively. If you received a range offer yourself, focus on the end that is favorable for you and treat the situation as if the other side had offered this specific number. Furthermore, assume that the others will go beyond this end point if needed to reach agreement.

Range offers are usually ineffective with competitive or adversarial negotiators, which includes Russians and Ukrainians, but also many Americans, Israelis, and others. The tactic works better in cultures where the concept of *face* is very important, such as China, India, Indonesia, Japan, Malaysia, or Singapore, since settling the deal within the range that was offered is a *face*-saving and therefore favorable outcome in these countries.

Written Offers

Rather than starting the bargaining exchange with a verbal initial offer, negotiators may instead present one in writing. It is essential to create professional looking documents for this purpose. Because of the perceived seriousness and legitimacy of written documents, the other side may find it psychologically harder to demand changes to such offers. In rare cases, they may even accept them as presented.

Should you receive a written offer yourself, remember that it does not give you any advantage over a verbal one, so treat it as if it had been made orally. After all, the fact that someone typed it up alone does not make the proposal any more deserving.

Making written offers is acceptable in all cultures, though not always useful. The technique may not show much effect, if any, in polychronic cultures such as France, most of Latin America, or in the Middle East. Since people in these countries tend to pay little attention to written documents, you may find during your initial discussion that they have not even read the offer, instead asking you to explain what it says.

On the other hand, written offers can be surprisingly effective in monochronic cultures, especially those whose members generally dislike bargaining, such as Australia, Austria, Germany, the Nordics, or Switzerland. People from these countries often prepare such offers themselves. The approach is also common in other monochronic cultures, for example the United States and Canada.

Written Terms and Conditions

At a late state in the bargaining exchange, when closure seems within reach, negotiators may suddenly produce pre-printed documents or forms introducing additional terms and conditions, such as contract processing fees or shipping costs. Three factors can make this approach effective: for one, just as with other written offers, it leverages the authority of printed documents, which many people find psychologically hard to challenge. In addition, since the new documents usually introduce numerous conditions and requirements, some clauses favoring the initiating party may go undetected. On top of that, the tactic can become a variant of *Limited Authority* (see page 124): negotiators introducing additional terms and conditions often claim that these clauses are imposed on them, usually by some unnamed higher authority, and that they are unable to make any changes.

Car dealers and real estate agents frequently use written terms and conditions. However, the tactic is also common in many professional business situations, such as with outsourcing service providers, energy suppliers, and many others.

If you detect attempts to introduce non-negotiable written terms and conditions into the negotiation process, insist that both parties agree that everything remains negotiable. Should your counterparts insist that they do not have the authority to make changes, simply ask them to pull in someone who does. More often than not, they will find ways to work around such clauses if the alternative is that the deal may be off.

This technique can be effective in the bargaining and closure phases of negotiations. Its greatest potential exists when dealing with strongly monochronic cultures whose members generally dislike bargaining, such as Australia, Austria, Germany, the Nordics, or Switzerland. Many of them use written terms and conditions themselves whenever feasible. The tactic can also be effective in other monochronic cultures such as the United States and Canada. Because people in these cultures are often rushed, they may prefer accepting last-minute additions over further delaying closure of the negotiation.

The approach is usually ineffective in polychronic cultures such as France, most of Latin America, or many Arab countries. People in these countries generally pay less attention and assign less authority to written documents. They may therefore insist on negotiating all terms and conditions individually.

Stalling

Negotiators attempting to 'buy time' sometimes resort to stalling tactics. This includes becoming unresponsive, requesting additional documents or time-consuming 'clarifications,' repeatedly demanding insignificant changes to aspects that had previously been agreed upon, and other actions designed to slow the negotiation process. Unlike with *Time Pressure* (see page 136), the objective is usually not to make the other side more conciliatory. Instead, negotiators using the approach may hope that external circumstances will change in their favor, for instance if other potential partners emerge or if market conditions improve. They might also need the additional time to re-evaluate their negotiation strategy, to obtain additional information about their counterparts, or for some other reason.

Stalling negotiations can be risky in countries where business is generally fast-paced, such as the United States and Canada. Members of these cultures often hate wasting time and may have little patience if they feel that the other party is hiding or holding back something. Worst case, they could lose interest in the deal. While business is usually conducted at a slower pace in other monochronic cultures, for example in Australia, Austria, Germany, the Nordics, or Switzerland, people there also dislike stalling and may react with persistent attempts to accelerate the negotiation process.

References

Acuff, Frank L. 1997. *How to Negotiate Anything With Anyone Anywhere Around the World*. New York: AMACOM.

Adler, Nancy J. 2002. *International Dimensions of Organizational Behavior*. Cincinnati, OH: South-Western.

Brake, Terence, and Danielle Medina Walker, Thomas (Tim) Walker. 1995. *Doing Business Internationally – The Guide to Cross-Cultural Studies*. New York: McGraw-Hill.

Cellich, Claude, and Subhash C. Jain. 2004. *Global Business Negotiations*. Mason, OH: South-Western.

Cialdini, Robert B. 2001. *Influence. Science and Practice*. Needham Heights, MA: Allyn & Bacon.

Cleland, David I., and Roland Gareis. 1994. *Global Project Management Handbook*. New York: McGraw-Hill.

Craver, Charles. 2002. *The Intelligent Negotiator*. New York: Prima Publishing

Curry, Jeffrey Edmund. 1999. *A Short Course in International Negotiating*. San Rafael, CA: World Trade Press.

Davies, Roger J., and Osamu Ikeno. 2002. *The Japanese Mind. Understanding Contemporary Japanese Culture*. Boston: Tuttle Publishing.

Deresky, Helen. 2003. *International Management – Managing Across Borders and Cultures*. Upper Saddle River, NJ: Prentice Hall.

Deutsch, Morton. 2000. *Cooperation and Competition*, in *The Handbook of Conflict Resolution: Theory and Practice*. Edited by Morton Deutsch and Peter Coleman. San Francisco: Jossey-Bass Publishers.

Devine, Elizabeth, and Nancy L. Braganti. 1986. *The Traveler's Guide to Asian Customs & Manners*. New York: St. Martin's Press.

Fisher, Roger, and William Ury. 1991. *Getting to Yes*. New York: Penguin Books.

Foster, Dean Allen. 1992. *Bargaining Across Borders*. New York: McGraw-Hill.

Foster, Dean. 2000-2002. *The Global Etiquette Guide to xxx'* series (4 volumes), New York: Wiley.

Gundling, Ernest. 2003. *Working Globesmart*. Palo Alto, CA: Davies-Black Publishing.

Hall, Edward T. 1981. *Beyond Culture*. New York: Anchor Books.

Hampden-Turner, Charles, and Alfons Trompenaars. 1993. *The Seven Cultures of Capitalism*. New York: Doubleday.

Hendon, Donald W., and Rebecca Angeles-Hendon. 1990. *World-Class Negotiating*. New York: John Wiley & Sons.

Hernandez Requejo, William, and John Graham. 2008. *Global Negotiation: The New Rules*. New York: Palgrave Macmillan.

Hofstede, Geert. 1997. *Cultures and Organizations. Software of the Mind*. New York: McGraw-Hill.

House, Robert J., and Paul J. Hanges, Mansour Javidan, Peter W. Dorfman, Vipin Gupta (editors). 2004. *Culture, Leadership, and Organizations – The GLOBE Study of 62 Societies*. Thousand Oaks, CA: Sage Publications.

Lam, N. Mark, and John Graham. 2006. *China Now. Doing Business in the World's Most Dynamic Market*. New York: McGraw-Hill.

Lewicki, Roy J., and David M. Saunders, John W. Minton. 2001. *Essentials of Negotiation*. New York: McGraw-Hill.

Lewicki, Roy J., and David M. Saunders, John W. Minton, Bruce Barry. 2003. *Negotiation*. New York: McGraw-Hill.

Lewis, Richard D. 1999. *When Cultures Collide*. London: Nicholas Brealey Publishing.

Nisbett, Richard E. 2003. *The Geography of Thought*. New York: The Free Press.

Morrison, Terri, and Wayne A. Conaway, George A. Borden. 1994. *Kiss, Bow, Or Shake Hands*. Holbrook, MA: Adams Media Corporation.

Morrison, Terri, and Wayne A. Conaway, Joseph J. Douress. 1997. *Dun & Bradstreet's Guide to Doing Business Around the World*. Paramus, NJ: Prentice Hall.

Putzi, Sybilla M. (managing editor). 2001. *Global Road Warrior*. Novato, CA: World Trade Press.

Rody, Raymond C. 2002. *International Business Negotiations*. Orange, CA: Oceanprises Publications.

Salacuse, Jeswald W. 2003. *The Global Negotiator*. New York: Palgrave Macmillan.

Seligman, Scott D. 1999. *Chinese Business Etiquette*. New York: Warner Books.

Schein, Edgar H. 2004. *Organizational Culture and Leadership*. San Francisco: Jossey-Bass.

Stewart, Edward C., and Milton J. Bennett. 1991. *American Cultural Patterns. A Cross-Cultural Perspective*. Yarmouth, MA: Intercultural Press.

Thomas, David C. 2002. *Essentials of International Management*. Thousand Oaks, CA: Sage Publications.

Thomas, David C., and Kerr Inkson. 2003. *Cultural Intelligence*. San Francisco: Berrett-Koehler Publishers.

Thompson, Leigh L. 2005. *The Mind and Heart of the Negotiator*. Upper Saddle River, NJ: Pearson Education, Inc.

Trompenaars, Fons, and Charles Hampden-Turner. 1998. *Riding the Waves of Culture*. New York: McGraw-Hill.

Trompenaars, Fons, and Peter Wooliams. 2003. *Business Across Cultures*. Chichester, England: Capstone.

Various authors. *Culture Shock!* series (available for more than 50 different countries). Singapore: Marshall Cavendish International.

Useful Websites

asia Travelinfo.com – www.asiatravelinfo.com

Austrade Industry and Country Information –
www.austrade.gov.au

Centre for Intercultural Learning / E-thologies –
www.e-thologies.com

Economist.com Country Briefings –
www.economist.com/countries/

Economist Intelligence Unit – www.eiu.com

Executive Planet – www.executiveplanet.com

HLB International 'Doing Business in ...' booklets –
www.hlbi.com/DBI_list.asp

International Business Center –
www.international-business-center.com

Kwintessential Country Profiles –
www.kwintessential.co.uk/resources/country-profiles.html

Negotiating International Business Country Sections –
www.leadershipcrossroads.com/nib_cs.htm

Transparency International Corruptions Perception Index (CPI) -
www.transparency.org/publications

U.S. Census Bureau – www.census.gov

U.S. Department of State Background Notes –
www.state.gov/r/pa/ei/bgn/

The World Bank – www.worldbank.org

The World Factbook – www.odci.gov/cia/publications/factbook

These links can also be found on the web at

www.negintbiz.com

In addition to the information provided on these web sites, several major international accounting, banking, and legal firms offer thorough and well-researched country-specific reports and forecasts. This research is often available to clients free of charge.

Index

Breinigsville, PA USA
13 March 2011
257544BV00006B/70/P